CRITICAL
VMWARE
MISTAKES
YOU SHOULD AVOID

LARRY LOUCKS

Brio Press
12 South Sixth Street #1250
Minneapolis, Minnesota 55402
www.briobooks.com

Manufactured in the United States of America

10 9 8 7 6 5 4 3 2 1

Book Design: Russell Boldt & Anthony Sclavi
Book Illustrations: Kelly Brown

ISBN 13: 978-1-937061-98-2
Library of Congress Control Number: 2011930663

Contents

Introduction

How NOT to Virtualize your Environment

It's been said "hind sight is 20/20." Whenever one takes on any project whether it's building a deck outside of your house, installing that new surround sound system for your home, making a repair to a car engine or virtualizing a network, there are always a number of items one finds they would do differently now that they have experience of the work to be performed and are more aware of the potential errors and pitfalls. They have "hind-sight" now, having walked the path so if they were to take on the same project again at a future point they would do some things differently having had the benefit that experience. Regarding virtualization, this book is your purchasable hindsight. The misconfigurations and mistakes identified in this book are taken from over 7 years of experience focused in the virtualization sector of the IT industry – including a couple of years with VMware in various capacities – by the author.

It's important to understand that this book does require some prerequisite knowledge. A basic understanding of the following concepts is necessary to fully understand everything written in this book:

1. VMware ESX server, vCenter and virtualization knowledge. This book is not designed to be a "virtualization 101" introduction to VMware. You must already have an understanding of virtualization and VMware to get the most out of this book. If you don't have this knowledge you can find affordable computer based virtualization training you can search www.amazon.com for "Professional vSphere Foundation" for a DVD course that will provide you with this information affordably. This book is designed to teach virtualization admins, IT managers and people who are working or will be working with virtualization, how to avoid common misconfigurations and mistakes.

2. Ethernet networking, IP addressing, MAC addresses, VLANs and switching (If you don't have this knowledge pick up a copy of Sybex Publishing's CCNA Study Guide)

3. Storage basics including VMFS volumes

As an Information Technology (IT) professional of 24 years, a former VMware Senior Consultant and someone who has specialized in virtualization for the past 7 years of my career, I have seen the same mistakes made over and over as companies attempt to virtualize their environment. In this book I share with you these common mistakes as well as best practices and proper configuration methods in the hopes that you will avoid making the same mistakes that many have. Virtualization is displayed as a veritable panacea. For most companies, it is: Simpler disaster recovery, easier deployment of new servers and applications, the ability to move VMs around on-the-fly with no interruption of service, improved ROI on purchased hardware and improved manageability. These are all part of the virtualization picture – *if you virtualize correctly.*

When an IT department doesn't virtualize their environment correctly, ("correctly" here defined as what works best in your environment with its own unique computing demands and needs and in accordance with accepted virtualization best practice), the results can range from annoying to catastrophic. My goal here is to provide principles and practices that can assist you in setting up your virtual environment correctly. Just one of the pitfalls described in this book, if avoided, can save your company huge amounts of wasted IT $$ and help you and your IT staff avoid the frustration of experiencing critical VMware mistakes you should avoid.

Happy Virtualizing!
Larry Loucks

Chapter 1

The Common Approach to Virtualization

There is a common path or approach to virtualization that occurs in almost every environment I've ever seen virtualize. In my travels I've worked in spaces ranging from single ESX server environments to global corporate headquarters and everything in between. In all these spaces I have seen this common path followed many times. See if this sounds familiar to you:

The Road Most Traveled

Here are the steps or phases many companies go through when virtualizing their IT environment:

1. Hear all the hype about virtualization
2. Check out the technology
3. Evaluate a virtualization platform (VMware has around 80%-90% market share by most estimates)
4. Begin to virtualize non-critical systems
5. Virtualize mission critical systems – PROBLEMS TYPICALLY START HERE

Let's take a look at each of these phases and see what sort of activity typically takes place in each.

Phase 1 - Hear all the hype about virtualization

What's that I hear? At this point one hears all the hype about virtualization (improved ROI on hardware, consolidation of servers, simpler disaster recovery, etc.) There is always a new gadget in the IT industry however virtualization is unique in that it's a ubiquitous technology. Whereas with other technologies "x"-amount of customers will adopt, with virtualization all of the major industry vendors have announced some sort of virtualization posture, initiative or product. I've told customers, "It's not a matter of deciding *if* you'll virtualize, it's a matter of deciding *when* you'll virtualize.

Phase 2 - Check out the technology

At this point we start looking into the technology through any number of means available to see if all we've heard is true. Maybe we attend some webinars, read through a ton of websites, visit a locally provided "show-and-tell" or attend the mother of all virtualization conferences – VMWorld – to see if all of the hype is true. What we usually find here are happy people with great reports about how wonderful virtualization works and then we decide we need to try this technology out for ourselves.

Phase 3 - Evaluate a Virtualization Platform

Next, we install some sort of virtual platform and begin to evaluate this technology in our environment. As of this writing VMware's ESX server and its management tool, Virtual Center (or vCenter as it's now called) have around 80%-90% of the enterprise marketshare so we will focus largely on that platform in this book with a few references and comparisons to others.

In this step we install some ESX servers and vCenter and begin to experience what it's like to work in a virtual environment. Before too long we're building new VMs in 10 minutes with templates and clones, we're moving VMs around on the fly with vMotion™ and setting up failover clusters among our ESX servers in 5 minutes or less. It doesn't take too much of this to see, this technology is cool stuff!

Phase 4 - Begin to Virtualize Non-critical Systems

After evaluating virtualization technology we get the green-light to virtualize our environment. We have ESX servers to build, P2V (Physical to Virtual) migration work to do, new VMs to create, and let's not forget a new disaster recovery (DR) project. Odds are, DR is the main reason we virtualized anyway. Industry studies have shown (and my travels and experiences confirm) that improved disaster recovery is the number one reason companies virtualize.

Easy stuff first – Most companies, when they virtualize, will start with the easy servers, the servers that aren't mission critical, relatively speaking, and the ones that won't generate a career change opportunity if they go down for a short period. Why? Two reasons: 1) We have to build our confidence in the technology, 2) We have to build confidence in our ability to manage the technology. It's one thing to talk about or read about virtualizing. It's a whole other issue to virtualize my IT shop. So, servers like DHCP, DNS, file servers, non-critical utility servers, all make good candidates for virtualization. These typically require relatively low use of computing resources (processor, network I/O, disk I/O and memory) and sometimes even have backup servers in the event of a failure. A backup DNS server would be an example of such.

Phase 5 – Virtualize Mission Critical Systems

Serious Virtualization, Serious Problems – In this phase companies will begin to attempt to migrate mission critical and/or computing-resource-intensive applications to the virtual environment. *This is often where the problems begin or, better stated, manifest.* If the virtual environment has not been implemented correctly at one or more points admins will often begin to experience problems in this phase. Poor VM performance and unhappy users is the end result but the root cause can vary wildly. **One of the most important concepts to understand is that virtualization is a completely new layer of infrastructure for your environment and troubleshooting that infrastructure requires a completely different approach than that which is required for troubleshooting a non-virtualized environment. This book is designed to help you prevent or eliminate these problems and gain some necessary understanding.**

I have seen companies, more times than I can recall, experience problems at this phase and "having been burned" as a few customers put it to me, adopt a very conservative posture towards virtualization. I've had many customers tell me the following in one way or another: "We're going to virtualize the low-hanging fruit – the easy stuff – but we're not going to virtualize any mission critical systems because they don't perform well." The tragedy is this is completely untrue. Thousands of companies all around the world have virtualized mission critical systems like Exchange, SQL and other key application servers successfully. The key here is understanding how the virtual environment works and setting that portion of your infrastructure up correctly. Besides, mission critical systems are where we most want to experience the benefits of virtualization – High Availability (HA), Distributed Resource Scheduler (DRS) for load balancing, improved disaster recovery – all of these things are most important for my more critical systems. It may not get noticed if a backup DNS server goes down for an hour or so but my Exchange server being down will definitely draw unwanted attention.

So, my recommendation: DON'T adopt a very conservative posture toward virtualization but DO take time to understand your environment and the best practices necessary to keep it running well. Odds are, if you're reading this book you're already on your way to doing the latter.

Virtualization Expertise and the Lack Thereof

I need to emphasize a previous point while making a new one here. As I mentioned earlier, your virtualization platform represents an entirely new infrastructure for your IT department to manage. You wouldn't install a Cisco router/switch infrastructure without taking some time to learn how to configure/troubleshoot that new infrastructure would you? If you did, what would you do when problems arose? If you had little to no understanding of how to connect to the switch or router and look around for key indicators of problems how could you resolve any issues with that equipment or its configuration?

In six years of field work focusing specifically on virtualization, I have found there are relatively few virtualization experts out there. Most industry studies have shown that despite the wild proliferation of virtualization technology during the past 5 years, still only about 40% of the market is virtualized. The reality is there are millions of servers out there and virtualization is still a relatively new technology in our industry. The number of Microsoft certified people for example, dwarfs the number of VMware VCPs in the industry simply because Windows has been around a lot longer. Eventually perhaps, we will reach the place in our industry when virtualization awareness is as common as Windows familiarity but as an industry we're not there yet. I speak to thousands via the web and onsite public speaking events each year and I've found, if I'm speaking at a VMware User's Group (VMUG) for example, and I ask, "How many here have heard of CPU %Ready values and understand how they affect performance of your virtual machines?" About 90%-95% will indicate they have never even heard of CPU %Ready values. If I ask, "How many understand VMKernel swap activity and how it is used by overcommitted ESX servers?" Usually around 80% haven't even heard of VMKernel swap. These are important indicators of health in a virtual environment. Understanding principles of how a virtual environment works is paramount in understanding these and other values in your virtual environment. This understanding is of course also necessary for rapid problem resolution.

With that said, taking time to understand how your virtual infrastructure functions is a key to maintaining a healthy virtual environment and this book is designed to assist in this matter.

Chapter 2

The Virtual Architecture and Shared Computing Resources

This book is all about identifying problem configuration situations on ESX server and helping you avoid common oversights and mistakes regarding ESX configuration. To do this we need to have an understanding of how ESX server allocates resources to, and shares resources among, VMs. With server performance there are always four key performance categories with which we concern ourselves: network I/O, memory utilization, CPU and storage (utilization and I/O). This chapter will provide a brief overview of each. The following chapters will dive deeper into each of these categories and show you how to avoid common misconfigurations.

In a non-virtualized server environment each server is an island. A single server hosts a single operating system and the operating system and applications on that server have exclusive access to all of the resources available to that server. The servers processors/cores, network cards, disk subsystem and storage space can all be used to capacity by the OS and applications on that particular box. Moreover in a non-virtual environment nothing moves. It is inherently a non-dynamic environment. Utilization levels are usually fairly static and predictable.

The non-Virtual Environment – Single Server, Single OS, Single Tier 1 Application

When we virtualize our environment all of this changes. Now many virtual machines (virtual servers) can reside on a single server. Each of these virtual machines has shared access to the available computing resources and no one virtual machine can monopolize any of the available resources. This is a good thing as it allows us to get more average utilization from our hardware and the ESX server OS prevents monopolization of resources by any one VM. These resource sharing mechanisms have to be understood to be properly managed.

The Virtualized Environment – Single Server (Host), Multiple Server Operating Systems per Host (Virtual Machines or VM's), Multiple Applications per Host

Also, virtual environments are inherently dynamic. VMs can and do move around, sometimes because of administrator actions and sometimes automatically. vMotion™, cold migrations and HA/DRS events can all move VMs around in your server environment. This means that utilization levels on servers can change drastically and quickly. We can also create new VMs in just minutes with templates and clones. All of these things create a dynamic, less-predictable environment than we had in a non-virtualized world.

With servers we have 4 primary resource concerns: network I/O, memory, disk (I/O and space usage) and cpu. Let's briefly discuss how each of these are shared in a virtual environment. *(Please note: The following are brief overviews. If you are unfamiliar with the ESX server and vCenter, search Amazon.com using "Professional Vsphere Foundation" for material which can be very helpful in providing detailed understanding of all of these topics. We will also go into more detail in later chapters.)*

Network I/O
ESX server hosts virtual machines with virtual network interface cards (NICs). These virtual NICs connect to virtual switches which are simply logical entities that provide a path or connection point from virtual NICs to physical network adapters. The physical NICs in ESX servers do not have IP addresses associated with them but rather act as pass-through mechanisms from the virtual NICs to the physical network.

Virtual machines with virtual NICs connected to virtual switches

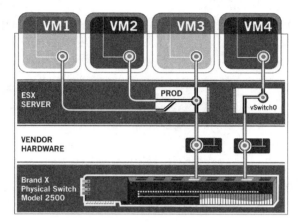

In a virtual environment IP addresses are associated with the Virtual Machine. Virtual Machines are prevented from monopolizing a network path through the use of proportional shares. Proportional shares in ESX server guarantees that during contention each virtual machine will be given access to the network. Shares are only enforced when there is contention for resources. If there is no contention, in other words if there are plenty of network resources with no conflicts, each VM is simply given what it needs.

In a single NIC environment the virtual machines and ESX server console all share access to the same network path. Again, if there is no contention, each simply gets what it needs. If there is contention, equal allocation of shares by ESX server to network I/O guarantees all VMs and the Service Console (SC) can communicate.

VMs and ESX Service Console Sharing the same physical NIC

If we add two or more NICS to a virtual switch ESX has a default load-balance mechanism that amounts to a round robin approach to load balancing. As an example, VM1 may use NIC1, VM2 – NIC2, VM3 – NIC1, VM4 – NIC2 and so on. This default methodology works fine for many environments but can end up with NICs carrying unequal loads.

VMs and ESX Service Console using multiple physical NICs

ESX can be configured to perform link aggregation which effectively uses a conversation-based load balance across the various NICs associated with a virtual switch. The Ethernet switch to which ESX is connected must support this and this method requires configuration on both the ESX server and the Ethernet switch.

Here we see several of the load-balancing options available to ESX server

Because the default load-balance methodology used by ESX is a round-robin approach to load balancing, if we add 2 NICs to a single virtual switch for use with a high network I/O application, the application will not be able to utilize both NICs by default. All transmissions from that VM will be associated with a single NIC. The second NIC will sit idle unless there is a failure of the first NIC. If we configure link aggregation however, the VM will gain the combined throughput of both NICs while maintaining the failover capability offered by multiple NICs.

Memory Usage in ESX Server

As we add VMs to an ESX server the total physical RAM in the server is available to the VMs minus a small amount for the Console Operating System (COS) and the VMKernel. The COS is loaded in the lower address pages of RAM while the VMKernel occupies the top address space. The space in between is available for VMs.

Memory in ESX can be overcommitted, that is to say we can assign more RAM to VMs on the server than the amount of RAM that physically exists. For example, if I have an ESX server with 32GB of RAM I can build VMs and assign more than 32GB total to all of the VMs

In many environments one can overcommit the ESX servers and "get away with it" if the VMs don't actually need all of the RAM assigned to them. This is because when a VM boots, ESX does not by default, allocate all of the RAM assigned to the VM when the VM powers on. With the default configuration, the VM gets half of its assigned RAM at power on. This behavior can be changed by adjusting the minimum memory assignment for the VM. If the VM needs more than half of its assigned RAM ESX can allocate more RAM as needed by the VM up to but not to exceed the max amount of RAM assigned to the VM.

If the ESX server is overcommitted for memory and the VMs actually need RAM in excess of the RAM available, there are several processes

ESX uses to keep the VMs up and running even though the host is over-committed. These processes include the proportional share mechanism, balloon driver activity and VMKernel swap file. ESX also uses shared RAM as a way of more efficiently allocating pages of RAM. We will discuss all of this in more detail in the chapter on memory.

CPU Utilization

Almost every week I talk with virtualized businesses who do not understand how ESX schedules virtual machines to processor. Many people I speak with don't realize that all of the VMs on their ESX server aren't necessarily all running at the same time. I thought one IT manager I spoke with recently was going to blow his top when he found out that VMs are scheduled to processor and sometimes they do not have access to processor. That's right. There are times in many environments when VMs literally do not have access to processor. Minimizing this time is a key to having a healthy virtual environment. When VMs aren't scheduled to a processor they are essentially paused or suspended.

This should be intuitive. Imagine you have an ESX dual socket/quad core server with 30 single vcpu VMs running on that host. There are only 8 cores. There is VM demand for 30 cores. Doesn't it make sense that they can't all be running at the same time? ESX server is effectively play-ing a very fast game of time-division multiplexing (read "virtual shuffle board") with VMs by scheduling them onto processor and then back off of processor, on demand.

Attention must be paid to how the VMs are scheduled onto proces-sor. One of the rules ESX server must obey when scheduling VMs to processor is that a VM cannot be scheduled to processor at all unless all of the cores are available to accommodate the vcpu assignment of that VM. In other words, if a VM has been assigned 4 vcpus, in order for ESX to schedule that VM to processor 4 cores must all be available at the same time. If we think about it this too should be a bit intuitive. If a guest operating system (the OS installed in the VM is called a guest OS) has been configured with 4 processors, ESX cannot just give it 2 proces-sors because that's what it happens to have available at this moment. The guest OS expects to see 4 processors all of the time.

This topic is what is referred to as CPU scheduling. Understanding this behavior is very important as CPU scheduling issues often create lots of problems in virtual environments and unless you know what to look for and where to look, the root cause of the problem can be very elusive. Fortunately we will give you all you need to know about CPU scheduling in this book.

Storage (I/O and Space Usage)

Our use of disk storage changes in virtual environments as well. Whereas in a non-virtual environment a single operating system usually had control of an entire disk sub-system or array, in a virtual environment we almost always end up using shared storage. Shared storage refers to storage volumes that are shared by multiple operating systems and VMs.

Here we see an ESX server with two different kinds of storage – a 136GB NAS (network) storage device and 73GB of local (internal to the server) storage device

View:	Datastores	Devices						
Datastores								
Identification	Status		Device	Capacity	Free	Type	Last Update	Alarm Actions
datastore1	⊘	Normal	Local DELL Disk (naa....	134.75 GB	118.84 GB	vmfs3	5/12/2011 3:42:15 PM	Enabled
LUN1	⊘	Normal	192.168.1.216:/LUN1	461.45 GB	452.29 GB	NFS	5/12/2011 3:42:15 PM	Enabled

Also, in a non-virtual environment an operating system is typically limited by the size of the physical disks or array to which it's connected. This too changes in a virtual environment. In a virtual environment we, as administrators, have to assign (read "guess") amounts of disk space to VMs. More often than not, IT departments in the industry use gross overallocation of disk space for VMs to allow for growth. This results in lots of wasted disk space in virtual environments. Later, we'll see more detail on this problem and some ways to avoid wasting storage space through overallocation.

Very rare is the VM that will max out the I/O capacity on contemporary storage. Remember however, that these days we use *shared storage*. This means many operating systems may be using the same local or storage area network (SAN) storage. Because of this we definitely can max out our SANs I/O capacity. Moreover, as we'll see later, many sites and SAN vendors do not configure storage in keeping with VMware best practices and through misconfiguration cause SANs to become "maxed out" long before the disks are full.

Troubleshooting and Problem Solving

Given all of these differences between the way non-virtualized systems and virtualized systems use available hardware, can you see why understanding these differences is absolutely necessary to troubleshooting, rapid problem resolution and root-cause analysis of the virtual environment? The most important pieces of knowledge you can possibly obtain as an administrator of a virtual environment are:

1. How your ESX hosts use and allocate resources
2. How to configure your environment in keeping with best practices
3. How NOT to configure your virtual environment (common mistakes)
4. For numbers 2 & 3, "Why?"

Chapter 3

Storage for Virtual Environments

Introduction

In this chapter we're going to discuss some basic concepts and practices regarding storage in virtual environments. As we will see, managing storage in a virtual environment has some unique twists and turns – some issues that we don't typically face with conventional, non-virtualized servers.

Some SAN vendors add performance enhancers and other features to attempt to deal with and/or avoid some of the issues I will describe in this chapter. That's fine but we should never design systems based upon performance enhancers. I will refer to general issues that are commonly true in this chapter along with good, old-fashioned best practices.

Also, in this chapter I'm going to share with you one of the most common and painful storage misconfiguration issues I've seen during my involvement in the virtualization industry. This storage problem is so common that I speak to customers almost every week that have this particular problem. When I was on the road for VMware, I saw this particular problem all of the time. Often, companies are completely unaware of this problem until long after they've purchased and configured their SAN. The particular problem I have in mind, in certain circumstances, can be "unfixable," depending on how the customer purchased their storage. I'm going to tell you about this common issue here *so you can avoid it.*

ESX Storage Basics

As mentioned in the Chapter 2 introduction to storage, in a non-virtual environment a single operating system usually had control of an entire disk sub-system or array. In a virtual environment we almost always end up using shared storage. Shared storage refers to storage volumes that are shared by multiple operating systems/VMs and often, by multiple ESX servers.

ESX servers contain virtual machines that have virtual disks. The virtual disks are files that *encapsulate* all of the files contained in the virtual machine. For example, imagine a traditional, non-virtualized server. This server has thousands or even perhaps hundreds of thousands of files stored on its hard drive. When we virtualize this server, all of these files become encapsulated in a single virtual disk file. Virtual disk files are noted by the their *.vmdk extension. By default, when we create a virtual machine, the .vmdk files (virtual disks) associated with that VM reside in the folder on the VMFS volume where we created the virtual machine.

VMFS Volumes

Most operating systems have their own type of volume format that they use. Over the years, for example, Windows systems have used FAT, FAT32 and NTFS volumes, just to name a few. ESX server is no exception to this common practice. ESX server volumes are formatted as a VMFS (Virtual Machine File System) volumes whenever we use local, iSCSI or Fiber Channel storage. NAS volumes are an exception to this rule. This are presented to the ESX server as an NFS network share or mount point. It is possible to have virtual machines use RDM's (Raw Device Mapping) which effectively points the VM to raw storage wherein the files are not encapsulated in a .vmdk file. RDMs are used in less than 1% of VMs and won't be part of our discussion in this book.

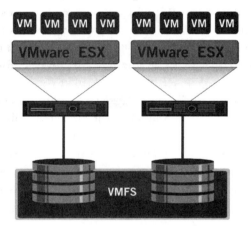

So, as we can see in the diagram above, the servers have the ESX server operating system installed and VMs run "on top of" ESX. These servers then connect to either local, iSCSI or Fiber Channel storage and the virtual disks are hosted on this storage in a VMFS volume. Recall NFS works similarly except that the storage is presented as a network share and is not formatted as a VMFS volume.

Local Storage

ESX servers can use local storage. Local storage can consist of disks connected directly to the server either installed internally in the server or externally through direct attached storage (DAS).

Local storage is usually only used in small ESX deployments. Since local storage is not shared among ESX servers, environments with only local storage cannot take advantage of VMware's High Availability (HA) or Distributed Resource Scheduler (DRS). DRS and HA require storage shared among your ESX servers. iSCSI, NAS and Fiber Channel-based storage are the three common types of shared storage

Shared Storage

Shared storage refers to storage systems that are shared among multiple ESX servers.

With ESX we can also use network storage in the form of Network Attached Storage (NAS) and iSCSI. These devices are typically used for light to moderate I/O environments respectively. One major concern with these technologies is that almost all of the iSCSI and NAS devices on the market ship configured as one large array and this is not changeable with many of them. This means that the creation of various LUNs on the array is just a façade. The ability to create LUNs simply designates an amount of space to a LUN for organizational aesthetics for humans, but in reality the entire storage device is a single large array. As such, when data is saved, it is striped across many or all of the drives in the array. Thus, the reads and writes of every VM in the environment impact many hard disks semi-simultaneously. Therefore the reads and writes of each VM affect the reads and writes of every other VM in the environment because they are all using the same disks simultaneously.

In order for a disk subsystem (local, iSCSI or Fiber) to host VMs, it is usually formatted as a VMFS volume. Network Attached Storage (NAS) devices are an exception to this. These are not formatted VMFS and are accessed through the NFS protocol and your network. Raw Device Mappings (RDMs) can also be used by the virtual machines for disk storage. RDMs are raw disk spaced that is used by a virtual machine. RDMs are only used in a small percentage of the industry's VMs however and I don't recommend using them unless there is clear reason from an application vendor to do so.

Also, in a non-virtual environment an operating system is typically limited by the size of the physical disks or array to which it's connected. This too changes in a virtual environment. In a virtual environment we, as administrators, have to assign (read "guess") amounts of disk space to assign to VMs. More often than not, IT departments in the industry use gross over-allocation of disk space for VMs to allow for growth. This results in lots of wasted disk space in virtual environments. Later, we'll see more detail on this problem and some ways to avoid wasting storage space through over-allocation.

Very rare is the individual VM that will max out the I/O capacity on contemporary storage. Remember however, that most virtualized IT departments use shared storage. This means many operating systems may be using the storage. *Because many OS's are sharing the same storage we have not only to think about consuming all of the space, but we also have to avoid maxing the I/O capacity of the individual disks in our arrays.* As we'll see later, many sites and SAN vendors do not configure storage in keeping with VMware best practices and through misconfiguration cause SANs to become "maxed out" long before the disks are full by exceeding the I/O capacity of the individual disks

The Risks of "Thin-provisioning"

There is much hype in the virtualization industry right now regarding software-based thin-provisioning of virtual disks. This feature of VMware's latest release, vSphere, is being talked about as if it were new, cutting-edge technology. In reality, thin-provisioning has been around almost as long as virtualization technology and isn't new at all. Thin-provisioning also carries with it substantial risks that can cause VM crashes and even corruption of data in certain circumstances.

During my time with VMware as a Senior Consultant, myself and the other Senior Consultants with whom I was familiar would *never* recommend a customer thin-provision any production systems because software-based, thin-provisioning can be a very risky approach to disk-space management. I personally engaged with a customer a few years ago that was utilizing a thin provisioning solution that accidently filled a LUN, crashed a bunch of VMs and corrupted thousands of files. It took them a week to get back up and running. Over the years I've spoken with numerous customers who have had similar problems.

Before we continue lets establish some key terms and definitions here just to make sure we're all on the same page.

Virtual Disk – A file that houses information for a virtual machine. The guest OS inside of the VM sees this file as a drive.

.vmdk (virtual machine disk) – the file type used by VMware's ESX server for virtual disks

Thick-provisioning – Thick-provisioned virtual disks are virtual disks for which all of the assigned disk space is allocated immediately as soon as the virtual disk is created. For example, if we build a VM and assign 100GB to the virtual disk, all 100GB of that space is allocated up front, even though there may be a much smaller amount of data actually residing in the virtual disk. As the amount of data associated with this VM grows and is saved in the virtual disk, the size of the .vmdk stays the same and data is saved into the virtual disk. The guest OS sees the size of the virtual disk as the total drive size. So a 100GB thick-provisioned virtual disk looks like a 100GB HD to the guest OS.

Thin-provisioning – Thin-provisioned virtual disks are virtual disks for which the assigned amount of disk space is NOT allocated at creation time. Only enough disk space is allocated to accommodate existing data with a small amount of additional "buffer" space. As more data is saved into the .vmdk ESX server will expand the .vmdk in increments of 16MB up to the maximum amount assigned to the virtual disk. The guest OS in the VM sees the max amount assigned to the virtual disk as the total drive size and is unaware the space isn't really allocated. So if a VM has 20GB of actual data and a 100GB, thin-provisioned virtual disk the guest OS sees a 100GB drive with 20GB of used space. The guest OS is unaware that only slightly more than the 20GB of space needed for data has been allocated.

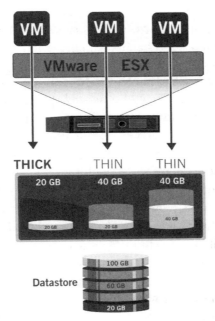

So, with these terms established, why is there so much hype in the industry regarding thin-provisioning? Why now? Is there a better solution?

Wasted Disk Space is the Problem

One of the issues we have in a virtual environment is that of wasted disk space. The reality is until recently the most commonly used method to handle disk space allocation to virtual machines was to grossly over-allocate the space. Let's see how this works.

In any server environment we can roughly divide all of the VMs into one of two types of systems:

1. VMs with which the users do NOT directly interact. The users do NOT save data to these systems. These tend to be fairly static except for the occasional service pack and expansion of log files. They usually require relatively small amounts of disk space. Many utility servers in the IT department such as DNS, DHCP and Active Directory Domain Controllers would be examples of these types of systems.
2. VMs with which the users DO directly interact. The users DO save data to these servers, they tend to be more dynamic and the growth rate is less predictable. These servers tend use larger amounts of disk space and are usually more critical servers. Examples of these would include file servers, mail servers, document servers and database servers.

Now let's take one of each of these types of VMs and discuss how disk space is typically allocated.

Example 1 (Type 1 VM – No direct saving of data)

Imagine we have a DHCP VM. The only thing that will ever run in this VM is Windows with the DHCP service enabled. The VM probably needs around 8GB of disk space plus a little extra for the occasional service pack or security update. Most IT shops would give the VM at least 20-40GB for drive C: even though they know they'll never use that much space. Why? Because ultimately the assignment of disk space to a VM is a best-guess on our part as administrators. We have to guess some amount of disk space that we believe will handle all of the patches, services packs, security updates, log files, etc. for the foreseeable future. Now, one might say, "Well the VM is only over allocated by 32GB, that's not that big a deal." True, but notice that we have allocated about 4X-5X the amount of disk space the VM actually needs. This over allocation times scores or hundreds of VMs in an environment equals lots of wasted space.

Example 2 (Type 2 VM – Users/Apps save data directly to these type of VMs)

Imagine we have a non-virtualized Exchange server that contains 25GB of data. We want to virtualize this environment and the question comes up "How much disk space should we assign the virtual disk for this new Exchange VM?" The reality is we have no idea how much disk space we will need. We have no idea how many service packs/security updates will come out for Exchange and Windows during the next couple of years. We have no idea how many emails and attachments this server will receive. True, we may be able to make vaguely educated guess if we are really familiar with the environment and typical growth/usage patterns in the environment but even this is a guess. So we have to guess some amount of disk space to assign to the VM. The only thing that is certain is that if we're smart about this we're not going to guess some conservative amount of disk space that will create a near-term problem for the VM. In other words I wouldn't take a 25GB Exchange server, virtualize it and give it a 30GB virtual disk so it will run out of disk space in four weeks and create a big fire drill in the IT Department as we scramble to expand the virtual disk, expand the partitions, get it all back up and running and explain to management how we got here in the first place.

So in an effort to avoid such a scenario most admins will assign some grossly over-allocated amount of disk space that they think will keep this VM running problem free for the foreseeable future, probably at least a couple of years. How do I know this? Well I know what I would do. Also of my 26 years in the IT Industry I've spent the past 7 working in the virtualization arena including contracting for VMware as an instructor and having been on staff with VMware as one of their Senior Consultants. I speak with thousands of virtualized customers every year in many different settings and I would say around 90% of the customers that I speak with are running thick-provisioned virtual disks that are over allocated to accommodate future growth. There really hasn't been a better way to deal with this. Perhaps in this example we would assign a 75GB-100GB virtual disk to this VM to accommodate growth in the VM. Notice once again we end up over-allocating by about 3X-4X.

What we end up with is that in many virtual environments the majority of allocated disk space is unused disk space. This means our SANs fill up more quickly therefore shortening the useful life of those devices and/or forcing IT Departments to purchase more disk space. Ultimately this waste leads to higher costs and a lower ROI for our investment in virtualization.

Introducing Thin-provisioning

Thin-provisioning is being touted as a way to avoid this waste of disk space, potentially lengthening the useful life of our storage and reduce storage-associated costs. Recall from our terms that in a thin-provisioned environment only slightly more than the used disk space is actually allocated. The .vmdk files can grow dynamically as needed and indeed, going with the industry statistic that about 50-80% of allocated disk space in virtual environments is unused disk space, one can definitely free up large percentages of storage space by implementing thin-provisioning. So what's the catch?

The Main Problem with Thin-provisioning

When a thick-provisioned virtual disk fills and someone tries to save data exceeding free-space, the error-checking mechanisms in the operating systems catch this and return an error (i.e. "insufficient disk space. Please move or delete files...."). When disks are thin-provisioned we effectively "lie" to the guest OS by implying it has disk space that isn't actually allocated. If the LUN unexpectedly fills and there are active, expanding .vmdk files, EVERYTHING may come to a screeching halt in these VMs.

Because the guest OS's cannot see the fullness or lack thereof on the VMFS volume, the error checking mechanisms in the operating systems do not catch the fact that the drive is full. The guest OS thinks it has room left on its "drive" but there is no space physically available for writing data.

All of the expanding, active VMs on that LUN have nowhere to go but down. There is no space to write a memory dump file, a log file, data or anything else. The VMs may instantly lock-up. Whatever data was partially saved is just that, partially saved. This can definitely corrupt data. If a LUN accidently fills in a thin-provisioned environment, VMs will almost assuredly crash. One additional inconvenience is that there is a performance hit for using thin-provisioning as the server continuously, dynamically allocated space on demand.

How Can a LUN Fill Accidently?

Many admins are unaware of other things that use LUN space in a virtual environment. Every time a snapshot is opened additional unplanned disk space is used for delta files. The first time every VM in their environment is booted a VMkernel swap file is created in accordance with the amount of RAM in the VM. This means if I have a LUN with 20 VMs at an average of 2GB of RAM each around 40GB of unplanned disk space is consumed for those swapfiles. Also, one of the characteristics of a virtual environment is its potentially dynamic nature. Things move around. Cold migrations, new VMs and SVMotion are all great opportunities to fill a LUN you weren't planning on filling.

My personal favorite is twice I have seen an ESX LUN fill because an admin somewhere in the building copied a bunch of ISO files to the LUN without looking to see if the space actually existed. FUN! FUN!

Now some admins might say "Well, I'll keep an eye on it." Really? In a completely dynamic virtual environment where people and processes are invoking snapshots, moving things around and provisioning new VMs? And let's not forget "John Doe" with the ISO files. "Keeping an eye on it" is a tall promise to keep for several years of operation in this dynamic, changing, growing environment and a stress/uncertainty I personally wouldn't want.

Keep in mind also that a LUN with plenty of space this morning may be out of space come lunch time. As one example, imagine we have a LUN hosting thin-provisioned virtual disks with 50GB of available disk space. At 8am this morning 50GB was available. At 10:30am an admin cold-migrated a 45GB VM to this LUN. Two hours later the LUN filled and crashed 15 VMs. Simply creating a VM on the LUN could provide the same effect.

Last but not least some might add "Well I'll setup alarms in vSphere that will let me know when critical thresholds of overcommitment occur." So what happens when you get down the road a few years, your SAN is fully near full capacity with virtual disks, your SAN has more data on it than expected, you're almost out of space and the VMs are thin-provisioned? At least with thick provisioned disks you can stop the growth while you plot a solution, and worst-case scenario, if a VM fills it just fills…no catastrophic crash across all VMs on the LUN and no corruption of data. The error checking mechanisms in the guest operating systems simply catch the fact that their drives have no more space. If that environment was thin-provisioned the potential for major data corruption definitely exists once the LUNs fill because invariably we will end up with partially-saved (read "corrupted") data.

Check out this article entitled "Don't Let Thin-provisioning Gotchas Getcha" at *http://www.networkworld.com/supp/2009/ndc1/012609-thin-provisioning.html.*

A Quote from the aforementioned article says :

> *"You've got to take the critical step of setting threshold alerts within your thin-provisioning tools because you're allowing applications to share resources…you can max out your storage space, and that can lead to application shutdowns and lost productivity because users can't access their data…You can get pretty close to your boundary, fast, and that can lead to panicked calls asking your vendor to rush you a bunch of disks."*

There are places where one can "get away with" using thin-provisioning fairly risk free. VMware Workstation is certainly a great place to use it. Small environments with low disk I/O intensity and low amounts of growth also may use it safely. Lab and dev environments can benefit from Thin provisioning as well simply because we can use less disk space to accommodate those environments. For production VMs with moderate – high disk I/O intensity and growth rates, I definitely recommend thick-provisioning.

Misconfiguration of Storage in Virtual Environments

The problem I'm about to describe for you is one that I consider to be the most common misconfiguration of storage in a virtual environment. Every year I speak with thousands of virtualized customers in various forums. Every month I speak with a customer who has been affected by what I'm about to describe for you. Often, by the time a customer realizes he/she has this problem large amounts of money have already been spent on storage that is inappropriate for their environment. Unfortunately, in the entire 7 years I've been working in this virtual space, I have never seen a reseller warn a customer about what I'm going to describe here. I suspect most resellers aren't aware of the issues I'm about to describe.

As I've mentioned, most virtualized environments chose to take advantage of some type of shared storage (NAS, iSCSI or Fiber Channel). First and foremost you must understand VMware's official recommendations regarding these storage types.

Low Disk I/O	**Moderate Disk I/O**	**High Disk I/O**
NAS	iSCSI	Fiber Channel

I'm familiar with the virtual infrastructure of one of the largest cellular companies in the world. They have multiple data centers. As you would imagine, a shop with thousands of VMs and a very busy network would definitely rank in the "high disk I/O" category. At this particular company they purchased fiber storage for one data center and – foolishly at the recommendation of a reseller – NAS storage for another one of their data centers. They have had nothing but problems with the NAS storage mostly because they didn't adhere to VMware's recommendations above and also because they aren't aware of what I'm about to describe.

Arrays and Storage Technologies

One distinguishing characteristic of the three types of shared storage mentioned in this chapter is how the arrays are configured on these various types of storage. Fiber storage typically allows the administrators to decide on array configurations. NAS and iSCSI storage options *usually do not allow administrators to have full control over array configuration.* As we will see this is a critical point in deciding which storage options are best for your business.

Allow me to introduce you to the Brand X Model 100 Fiber Channel Storage Array

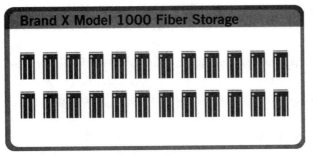

The Brand X Model 100 Fiber Channel Storage Array contains 24 hard disk drives of your choice, if all drive bays in the chassis are populated. Because this is a fiber channel array, you as the administrator, get to decide whether or not you want to format all of the drives as a single large array or separate the various drives into multiple arrays of varying RAID characteristics. RAID stands for Redundant Arrays of Inexpensive Disks. As mentioned earlier in the book this is not a server 101 or virtualization 101 book and we won't take time here to explain RAID arrays. If you're not familiar with RAID configurations and arrays there are many fine websites and books that can help you along. Be sure to familiarize yourself with RAID 1, 5, 10 and 15 at a minimum.

Fiber channel storage almost always consists of a chassis that can be populated with various types of drives. The drives can usually vary by size and/or spindle speed according to the administrator's preferences. Most importantly with fiber channel storage the administrator can decide how to setup the arrays across these drives.

For examples consider the following example of how our Brand X Model 1000 Storage might be configured:

Example A – Multiple Arrays in a Single Chassis

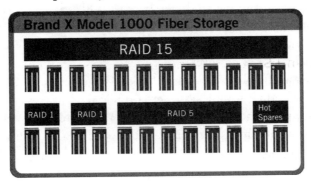

Notice in this configuration the drives in the Model 1000 have been broken up into separate arrays of varying RAID characteristics. The First 12 drives are configured as a Raid 15 Array. Next we see two separate RAID 1 arrays followed by a RAID 5 array and a couple of "Hot Spares" in the chassis.

It's important to note that as we format this storage as VMFS and begin to create virtual machines on these arrays that *the impact of VM storage I/O is limited to the arrays upon which the VM is installed.* In other words, if I place 10 virtual machines on the RAID 15 array those VMs are striped across the drives in that array *only*. Therefore the disk I/O of those 10 VMs is limited to the 12 drives in that array. The other drives would not be impacted at all by that VM activity since they are separate arrays. This, by the way, is part of what is considered VMware best practice as we'll see in a bit.

Example B – Single Large Array

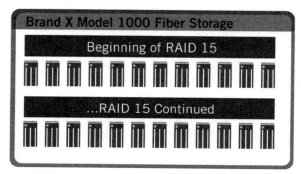

In example B we see the same storage device but in this case the device has been configured as a single large RAID 15 array. Since this device has been formatted as a single array, as I create LUNs and VMFS volumes and begin to install virtual machines on this storage array the VMs and all data are striped across all disks (or at least many depending on size). This means since the VMs are striped across all spindles the I/O activity of each VM affects all spindles. This is not to say each file read or write impacts all drives, because a file may be very small for instance, taking up only a few blocks therefore a read or write to that file may only impact a few spindles. The total activity of each VM however, does impact all disks however.

This means if I place 20 VMs on this storage device all 20 VMs will be striped across all spindles (or perhaps just most if the VMs are very small). The read and write activity of all VMs affects all spindles and therefore the combined workload of all VMs impacts all drives in this array.

Single Large Arrays, oh my!

Most iSCSI and NAS devices in the industry come configured as a single large array and this cannot be changed on many of these devices. Fiber storage systems can typically be broken into multiple arrays but very often the resellers or admins will provision the entire storage system as a single array.

Your SAN management software will allow you to carve our LUNs (Logical Unit Numbers) which are logical designations of storage. This can often be done regardless of how the arrays are physically setup.

Let's take another look at our Brand X Model 1000 storage device again.

Example C – Multiple Arrays of varying RAID characteristics, separate corresponding LUNs

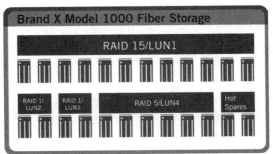

Notice in example C that the storage device is broken into multiple arrays. Notice also that our LUN designations map to the various arrays. This means we have arrays/LUNs of different RAID characteristics and sizes. Once again, because these arrays/LUNs are separate the activity of each LUN only impacts the drives that make up that LUN. Therefore if we place 10 VMs on LUN 4, the I/O of those 10 VMs will only impact the 6 drives in that array/LUN. Let's take a look at another approach to dividing and using storage.

Example D – Single large Array, multiple logical LUNs

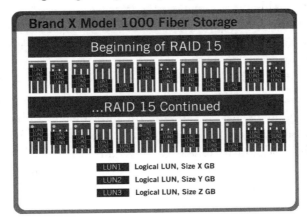

Notice now that our Brand X Model 1000 storage device is setup as a single large RAID 15 array. Three logical LUNS – LUNs 1-3, each of various sizes, have been created on the device. Note however that these are logical LUNs only. They don't map to separate arrays of drives but rather, since they were simply carved out logically from the single large array, these LUNs are striped across the various drives in the large RAID array. How they are striped in actuality would depend on the RAID type chosen.

So, let's imagine we take 10 VMs and drop them into LUN1. In the previous example C LUN 1 corresponded to 12 drives in the storage device. Therefore placing 10 VMs on LUN1 in example C would only impact the 12 drives that were a part of that LUN. Now however, in Example D, because the LUNs are striped across all drives logically, dropping 10 VMs in LUN 1 will impact all spindles since the LUN itself, and therefore the VMs, are striped across all spindles.

What's the Point?

The point is, if your storage device is allocated as a single large array physically, the creation of "LUNs" via your SAN management software is just for organizational/administrative purposes. The reality is each LUN impacts all drives. In Example C, because we divided the storage into separate arrays and then matched our LUN designations to the physical arrays, each LUN was truly separate. The I/O of the VMs in each LUN was *isolated to that LUN only*. By contrast, in Example D, the *I/O of each VM impacts each drive.*

The Key Piece of Information

Many customers, when purchasing storage, focus primarily on the amount of storage and expandability of that storage. Some customers consider the Input – Output capabilities of the storage device (expressed as I/Ops and called "iops" by many in the industry). The key however is that *each individual disk in a storage array has a discreet, max amount of I/O it can handle at any given time. In other words, each drive has a max I/Ops rating.*

The Secret

In a storage array, if the combined workload of all of the activity in that array exceeds the max IOps rating of the individual disks massive slowdowns can occur.

Recall our Example D where all LUNs are striped across all spindles. As I add more VMs to LUN 1 the combined workload of those VMs impacts each physical disk. When the workload begins to exceed the

IOps rating of the individual disks, buffers start to fill, retries may occur and all sorts of fun storage latency can occur. Note that this slowdown can be across the entire storage system and therefore affect all VMs.

Classic Symptoms and Examples

I speak with customers almost every week that have this problem in their environment and don't realize it. They may realize they have poor performance, but don't realize that it is their storage setup that is causing the problems.

The classic symptom of this problem is as follows: a customer purchases their storage array, uses it for some amount of time, adding VMs to the device. At some point, maybe 6 months, maybe a year down the road, the entire VM environment begins to perform very poorly. This can happen long before the storage device is "full."

Client Example 1

A large school in Florida a few years ago, purchased nice new server hardware and iSCSI storage. Like most iSCSI devices the storage was formatted as a single large array and *this could not be changed as is the cast with many iSCSI devices.* The customer loved the device initially. Through around 15 VMs the storage array performed wonderfully. At about 18 VMs they began to have occasional, unexplained VM slow-downs (helpdesk phone ringing). By the time they reached 25 VMs the storage device was practically unusable (read "department heads scream-ing and yelling/helpdesk phone ringing" – unusable). The combined workload of all the VMs had exceeded the max IOps capabilities of the disks in the storage unit and the customer, quite simply put, was hosed. Unfortunately, they had used less than 30% of the capacity in the stor-age device. Nonetheless, the box couldn't handle their workload. The customer had to back VMs off of that storage array until they got down to around 15 VMs to keep it running optimally. All of that extra space would never be usable to them. How would you like to go to your boss and say, "Remember that storage unit we just purchased 6 months ago? Well, it's far from full but we need more storage."

Client Example 2

I was in Richmond, VA a few years ago where a large IT organization dumped a ton of money into (what was then state of the art) top-brand servers and storage. The storage arrays they purchased were filled with the largest (which doesn't usually mean the fastest) drives they could buy. They spared no expense on this system. Their storage devices were all fiber channel so they had the option of breaking the devices into multiple arrays of varying RAID characteristics. Unfortunately, when the systems engineer from the manufacturer came onsite, he formatted the storage as single large arrays in each chassis.

I went onsite to do a VMware jumpstart and I began to notice that simple things, like spawning a 20GB Windows 2003 VM from a template, would take 45 minutes (it should have taken around 8 minutes). Because I've seen this so many times and therefore I knew to look for it I began to ask questions about their storage. I found out that while we had 3 LUNs carved out for our jumpstart that those LUNs were on the arrays I described above. These arrays had many other LUNs designated and lots of production virtual machines on them. Not only was the storage unbearably slow for our jumpstart but their production systems were performing really poorly and no one could figure out why.

This customer had Terabytes of data. They had also retired their old storage array. The only way to fix this fiasco is to move all of the VMs and other data off of the storage, reprovision the storage according to VMware best practices, move all of the VMs and data back, and recreate all of the VM virtual disk mappings in vCenter. Trust me, this makes for a very, very long weekend in the data center. Besides this, their conundrum was "What are we going to do with all these Terabytes of data while we fix this?" It's a good point. Most of us don't have Terabytes of unused or extra storage lying around.

So what is the best practice?

First of all remember industry best practice as outlined earlier:

Low Disk I/O	Moderate Disk I/O	High Disk I/O
NAS	iSCSI	Fiber Channel

Second, you must understand VMware's recommended method for allocating storage. VMware best practices call for using 2 types of LUNs – adaptive LUNs and predictive LUNs.

Adaptive LUNs are designed to hold several – many low disk I/O VMs. Low I/O utility VMs, DHCP VMs, DNS servers, etc. would all be likely candidates for these types of LUNs. Their size can be whatever you want it to be with the main consideration being simply "give the LUN enough space to accommodate the VMs we want to place there." Add VMs to the LUN and monitor performance through your SAN management software to make sure you're keeping the LUN utilization under the max IOps rating for the disks.

Predictive LUNs are LUNs that are created for moderate to high disk I/O VMs. These LUNs should be appropriate size and RAID characteristic for the application. Imagine a busy application server. The application vendor recommends a mirrored (RAID1), small drive C for the OS and application and a 200GB RAID 1 drive D for its database. So using the Predictive LUN scheme we could create this in our fiber channel SAN. We could place 2 inexpensive drives as a mirrored pair in the storage chassis and 2 high-speed SCSI drives as another mirrored pair for the data store. With this configuration the high I/O of this busy application server is isolated to the arrays we created for it. The I/O for this VM therefore doesn't impact the other VMs and drives and the I/O from the other VMs does not reduce performance of this application server.

Example E – This is an example Predictive LUN layout. LUNS of appropriate size and RAID characteristics service a single virtual machine. This guarantees best performance.

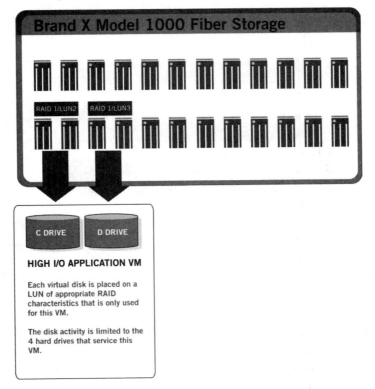

What if my storage device cannot be broken into multiple separate arrays?

This is a great question. Most iSCSI and NAS devices allow only a single RAID characteristic with all of the drives in the storage device participating in a single large array. We can use the vendor's SAN management software with these types of devices to setup multiple LUNS but again, with this type of storage device the creation of LUNs is really just for administrative organizational purposes. For many of these types of devices the LUN, and therefore the VMs in the LUN, are striped across many drives. This works fine as long as you're not maxing out the IOps on the individual disks. When you do, slowdowns across the entire system can occur.

If you have a storage device that can only be configured as a single large array there is one thing you can do to improve performance and possibly, the usable life of the SAN. That thing is proper alignment.

Storage Alignment

In a most virtual environments there are 3 "layers" of storage with which we are concerned. Physical Disk > VMFS/.vmdk > Guest OS Partition. This can be depicted as follows.

Example F – "Layers" of storage in a virtual environment

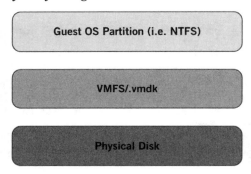

These various layers can be misaligned. Misalignment can occur between the virtual disk blocks (.vmdk) and the underlying physical disk blocks. We can also experience misalignment between the guest OS partition and the underlying virtual disk. Misalignment equals degraded performance. Having a misaligned environment can increase the number of IOps required to accomplish the workload in your environment. Properly aligning the environment can improve performance, decrease IOps to the storage device and extend the usable life of your SAN.

To ensure alignment between the VMFS volume and the underlying physical disk, create your VMFS volumes with the VI Client in vCenter.

There are several companies that make software to properly align the guest OS partition to the .vmdk. Some guest operating systems install into the VM properly aligned. Quest software, for example, has a free scanning tool called the vOptimizer Pro Wastefinder that can determine if/where you have misalignment.

Other than this, it's best to determine before you buy such storage devices if they can handle the IOps requirements in your environment. It doesn't hurt to try to obtain some guarantees to that effect from the vendor.

Conclusion

I heard it said recently that "thin-provisioning is a way for storage admins to write bad checks." I totally agree. This provisioning has the potential to create resume-generating events in your IT department staff.

Some say the solution is thin-provisioning more alerting to let you know when a train is coming. I say stay off the tracks and avoid thin-provisioning problems altogether by using thick provisioning. Software-based, thin-provisioning is being spoken of as if it's some new technology. The reality is it's not new, has been around for years and has risks of which admins need to be aware. On top of all of this thin provisioning doesn't perform as well as thick provisioned virtual disks, especially for disk I/O intensive applications.

When you consider a storage purchase don't just look for available space/expandable space. Make sure the device is appropriate for your environment according to recommendations listed in this chapter. Also make sure it can handle the workload in terms of I/Ops for your environment. Purchasing storage that allows you to break the device into multiple separate arrays gives you much more flexibility, allows for higher combined workload and allows for implementation of predictive and adaptive LUN schemes as outlined by VMware.

Chapter 4

Networking for Virtual Environments

Chapter Introduction

In this section we will review networking in virtual environments. Once again we will take time to understand principles of networking in virtual environments and then compare how NOT to properly network your environment with best practices – how to properly setup networking for your ESX environment.

This chapter does require some prerequisite knowledge to fully understand it. A basic understanding of Ethernet networks, switches, VLANs, IP addresses and MAC addresses are all desirable for this chapter. If you don't have knowledge of these components of a network I recommend a book published by Sybex entitled CCNA Study Guide. The information in that book is essential to proper management of the networking aspect of virtualization.

There will be a lot of "real-world" material and examples here. One factoid we'll reveal is so super secret you probably wouldn't be able to find one guy in a hundred that understands it. Let's carry on!

How Virtual Networking Works

There are a few basic architectural components we need to understand in order to grasp how networking works inside of an ESX server. These components are the Virtual NIC, the Virtual Switch (vSwitch), ESX Host NIC and the physical ethernet switch through which our ESX hosts connect to gain access to our company network. These components can be logically depicted as follows:

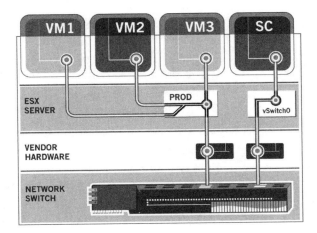

Here is how this relationship looks in the vCenter interface:

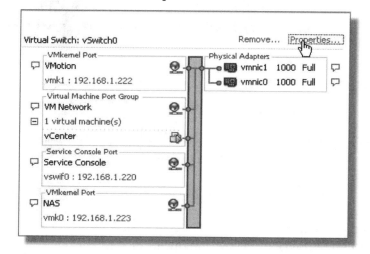

Virtual NIC – This is the NIC installed inside of the VM itself. Remember, when we virtualize, ESX server presents generic hardware to the Guest's operating systems and the Guest OS's "see" it as real hardware. The Virtual NIC will have an IP address assigned to it that is appropriate for that particular VM.

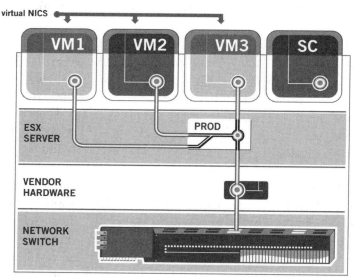

Virtual Switch – A Virtual switch is a logical entity (as opposed to a physical switch) that exists inside of the ESX server simply because we define it. In the picture we see two virtual switches, one named PROD and the other named vSwitch0. Virtual switches are named by admins and the names are case-sensitive so a vSwitch named Prod is not the same as one named PROD.

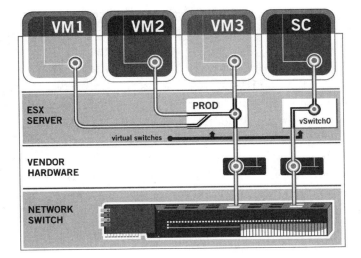

ESX Host NIC – This is the physical NIC installed inside of the ESX server. Unlike a NIC in a physical, that is to say non-virtualized, server, these NICs have no IP address assigned to them.

Ethernet Switch – This of course is the device to which you connect your ESX server to get physical connectivity to the network.

Putting it all Together

So how do all of these components work together? As soon as we build our ESX servers we create virtual switches inside of these servers and assign 1 or more physical NICs to the virtual switches. Note that you can create a virtual switch with no outbound NICs. This is called an internal-only virtual switch. If we add more than 1 physical NIC to a virtual switch, ESX server automatically does failover and load-balancing across those NICs. It's important to understand that this is NOT a true, statistical load-balance. Rather, it is a semblance of load balancing, a round-robin approach to load-balancing. We'll see more on this later.

Next we build our virtual machines. When we do so we assign IP addresses to the virtual NICs inside of the VMs and assign the virtual NICS to whichever virtual switch we chose. Confused yet? Let's take it from the VM and work down through the infrastructure all the way to the physical switch.

VM Virtual NIC > Virtual Switch > Physical NIC > Ethernet switch

Now if you understand the prerequisite material for this section you know that IP addresses get you to the network but ultimately the MAC address gets you to the individual device. In the scenario depicted above it's important to understand that the ESX host NICs are just *pass-throughs*. These NICs have no IP addresses assigned to them and their physical MAC addresses are not visible to the switches. IP packets have source and destination IP and MAC fields. The ESX server never serves as the source in this model, the virtual machines are the source. So, we know we can assign an IP address to the VM virtual NICs but how do we get the required MAC address to get network traffic to the VM itself? Simple! We make one up...well ok we don't, but ESX server does. When we create our VMs and give them a virtual NIC ESX uses an algorithm to generate a MAC address for the VMs. The algorithm helps guarantee the MAC address it generates will be unique. The MAC address for each VM is stored in the .vmx file in the folder on the VMFS volume where the VM resides.

So, as VMs send packets through the network the source IP and source MAC is associated with and sent from the VM, not the ESX server. Once again, the ESX Host NICs are simply pass-throughs to the network. As the packets come to the Ethernet switch, the source IP and MAC fields are populated with information from the VM *not* the ESX host.

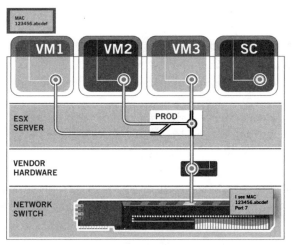

So the Ethernet switch associates the VM's MAC address with the physical port in which it received the VMs IP packets.

Network Load Balancing in ESX Server

Before we begin discussing how NOT to properly network your virtual environment, as well as how to properly network the environment, we need a quick review of load-balancing and NIC teaming in ESX server.

Recall that administrators create virtual switches, which are simply logical, named entities, and associate them with physical NICs. One of the great things about ESX server is that we can associate multiple physical NICs with a virtual switch and ESX server will automatically do load balancing and failover across these various NICs. It is important to understand however, how the load balance works. The default load balancing used by ESX server is not a statistical load balance. ESX server is not looking at multiple NICs and attempting to keep traffic levels somewhat even. Rather, the default load balance is effectively a round-robin approach to load balancing.

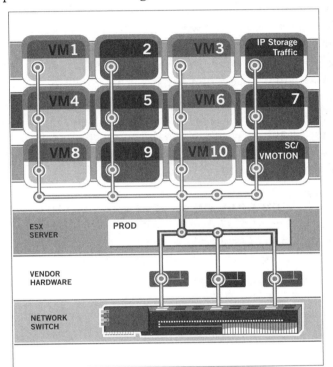

Virtual Switch load balance configuration
(each VMs traffic statically associated with a physical NIC via an algorithm)

VM1	-	Physical NIC1
VM	-	Physical NIC2
VM3	-	Physical NIC3
VM4	-	Physical NIC1
VM5	-	Physical NIC2
VM6	-	Physical NIC3
VM7	-	Physical NIC1
VM8	-	Physical NIC2
VM9	-	Physical NIC3
VM10	-	Physical NIC1
SC/VMotion	-	Physical NIC2
IP Storage Traffic	-	Physical NIC3

Here's how it works: Imagine an ESX server with 3 physical NICs that are associated with a single virtual switch. Connected to this virtual switch we have 10 virtual machines. ESX server will associate individual VMs with a NIC attached to the virtual switch. It uses an algorithm to do this, the detail of which we won't go into here but each VM's traffic is statically associated with a particular physical network card. This is true not only for VMs but also for Service Console, VMotion™, and IP Storage traffic if we just toss it all haphazardly on the same virtual switch(s).

Notice that each VM and various management components each have their traffic associated with a single NIC. What about failover? Well, if NIC1 were to go down in this scenario, for whatever reason, ESX server would use the algorithm to take the traffic that was associated with NIC1 and move that traffic to one of the remaining 2 NICs. Note that the order of association here (VM1 with NIC1, VM2 with NIC2, etc.) is arbitrary and simply an example. The algorithm that ESX server isn't so simplistic but the effects are the same – each VM's traffic and management traffic type is associated with a particular NIC.

How NOT to properly setup your virtual networking

1. Toss NICs in a server, associate them with a virtual switch and start piling on the functionality.
2. Add VMs to virtual switches with no understanding or review of network workload requirements and hope for the best
3. Add all management traffic (Service Console, vMotion™, etc.) to the same virtual switches, NICs and VLANs as your virtual machine traffic and let it all play together
4. Place your IP storage on the same virtual switches, NICs and VLANs as everything else because setting it up that way is so much easier
5. Have large, flat, switched VLANs that are far in excess of industry recommended sizes so the broadcasts of everything affect everything else on the network
6. Avoid using strict access lists to keep user traffic off of management VLANs

How NOT to properly setup your virtual networking – Item 1

Toss NICs in a server, associate them with a virtual switch and start piling on the functionality.

Think about the picture above. Knowing what we know now about how ESX network functionality works it should become obvious that with this default load balance methodology one could find one's self in a situation where the load placed on the various physical NICs could be wildly out of balance. We could end up in a situation where NIC3, for example, carried a much heavier traffic burden than the other 2 NICs because it is also hosting the storage traffic. We could also have a scenario where a couple of virtual machines associated with a particular physical NIC had a disproportionately high amount of traffic – relative to the other VMs on the ESX host. This would cause the physical NIC with which they were associated to carry a much higher average traffic load than the other 2 NICs.

Rare is the server or VM that with a single operating system and application set will max out a gigabit NIC. When we start piling lots of virtual machines on single NICs however, and adding storage and management traffic, we can definitely start maxing out NICs. This is something we have to be cognizant of in a virtual environment. Taking all VMs and traffic types, associating them with a single vSwitch and tossing some NICs in the mix is definitely an easy way to setup your environment, but it's not the best way that's for sure.

If you set your environment up in this way and toss all of this functionality on the same NICs and same IP VLANs all of the broadcast traffic from each service is going to impact available bandwidth of everything else.

- Spikes in activity may over-capacitate NICs resulting in retrys and delays.
- Mission critical applications that are network I/O intensive may not get adequate access to bandwidth.
- IP Storage performance may suffer if it cannot get adequate access to the network, especially during peaks in activity.
- Management traffic may intermittently suffer resulting in failed VMotion™ or poor VM console performance (VM console access passes through the service console NIC).

So, to address How NOT To – Item #1 – Please don't toss NICs in a server, associate them with a virtual switch and start piling on the functionality.

How NOT to properly setup your virtual networking – Item 2

Add VMs to virtual switches with no understanding or review of network workload requirements and hope for the best.

In virtual environments we have a new concept that becomes very important: relative utilization. Before we virtualized an OS and its few applications monopolized an entire server. Now that we've virtualized our environment we have implicitly turned servers, memory, CPU, storage and network access into shared resources. Now many VMs reside on the same server along with storage traffic and management traffic.

In an average IT environment most VMs won't use a particularly large amount of CPU, but some will. Most VMs won't use an inordinate amount of disk I/O, but some will. Most VMs will not use huge amounts of RAM or network I/O, but some will. We need to understand the relative utilization of the various VMs in our environments so we can properly access resources.

For example, since we're talking about networking in this chapter, imagine a company with 100 VMs. If you look closely at the network utilization on all 100 VMs most, perhaps 90 we'll say, use very little network I/O. Ten of them however have a much higher relative utilization of the network than do the other 90. We look closely and find that these 10 servers are a busy mail server, some app servers and a very busy document server.

If we use the default load balancing methodology these VMs and even several of these unusually network I/O intensive VMs could end up assigned to the same NIC. During spikes inactivity this may cause performance issues with the VMs, packets are dropped and retries take place. What makes this fun to troubleshoot (yes, I'm being sarcastic) is that these slowdowns or interruptions in service may be intermittent. The help desk phone rings, a user is complaining of poor performance and by the time someone looks into the issue 30 minutes later, there may be no problem

You need to take time to understand which VMs are resource intensive for each of the four major server resources in your environment – CPU, RAM, network I/O and disk I/O. I don't recommend trying to do this manually by looking at raw performance metrics. First of all, even if you check network I/O on a VM right now and see that it is low, that doesn't mean that it always runs that way. We're looking for average utilization and baselines here. The only way to do this reliably is through the use of good quality performance monitoring tools made specifically for virtual environments.

Once you understand the relative network I/O of your VMs, and understand which VMs makeup that small percentage that are very busy, relative to the others, you can properly design your networking environment according to facts and best practices. We will talk about how to do this later.

So, to address How NOT To – Item #2 – Please do not add VMs to virtual switches with no understanding or review of network workload requirements and hope for the best.

How NOT to properly setup your virtual networking – Item 3

Add all management traffic (Service Console, VMotion™, etc.) to the same virtual switches, NICs and VLANs as your virtual machine traffic and let it all play together.

It is always a best practice to keep management and storage traffic isolated from each other, user traffic and server traffic. As mentioned earlier tossing all of this functionality onto the same NICs via ESX server's default load balance methodology can result in the following undesirable situations:

- Broadcast traffic from each service is going to impact available bandwidth of everything else.
- Spikes in activity may over-capacitate NICs resulting in retries and delays.
- Mission critical applications that are network I/O intensive may not get adequate access to bandwidth.
- IP Storage performance may suffer if it cannot get adequate access to the network, especially during peaks in activity.
- Management traffic may intermittently suffer resulting in failed VMotion™ or poor VM console performance.

VM console access happens through the service console NIC, not the NIC associated with the VMs traffic. If we isolate critical management traffic through the use of VLANs we reduce bandwidth competition and the negative impact of broadcasts and other undesirables upon our management functions.

In this scenario it is possible to have everything suffer at the hands of everything else. VMs may get inadequate throughput because of excessive storage communications. Storage may perform inadequately because of bandwidth constraints or spike in VM activity. Console access may prove sluggish during spikes in activity as well.

So, to address How NOT To – Item #3 – Please do not add all management traffic (Service Console, VMotion™, etc.) to the same virtual switches, NICs and VLANs as your virtual machine traffic and let it all play together.

How NOT to properly setup your virtual networking – Item 4

Place your IP storage on the same virtual switches, NICs and VLANs as everything else because setting it up that way is so much easier

Naturally IP storage technologies like iSCSI and NAS rely upon available bandwidth and proper network design to function well. Clearly storage needs on demand, as-fast-as-possible access to the network. Using separate physical NICs and VLANs can help guarantee strong IP storage performance.

IP storage solutions should be place on isolated VLANs to guarantee performance and provide security to the storage devices themselves. You'll notice we're not talking about LUN sizing and design or disk I/O requirements here. Those items will be discussed in another chapter. In this chapter we're concerned with ESX and virtual networking so our focus at present is not disk I/O per se, but rather how to best position your IP storage on the network.

How NOT to properly setup your virtual networking – Item 5

Have large, flat, switched VLANs that are far in excess of industry recommended sizes so the broadcasts of everything affect everything else on the network.

What I'm about to tell you now could save your life. Well ok, probably not your life but your job. Ok, If not your job, at least your network performance. I personally have used the information I'm about to provide to radically improve network-wide performance on several corporate networks. One company I worked with, in Nashville, TN, brought in big dollar consultant groups, spent tons of money on hardware upgrades and ultimately still had very poor network performance and intermittent problems with disconnects, data corruption and overall slow servers/PCs. I visited them for a 4 day engagement, noticed they had this problem and showed them what had caused them so many problems for years. When I showed their lead admin what was going on I literally thought the guy was going to cry. He told me, "Our VP has spent tons of money trying to figure this out. He's about ready to start firing people over our performance problems."

This mistake involves admins having huge, flat, switched networks with one or very few VLANs. By "flat" I refer to the fact that there is no VLAN division of the IP network. Industry-leading network infrastructure vendors have recommendations for maximum number of devices per single VLAN. These recommendations differ slightly by vendor but 250-300 devices max per single, flat, switched VLAN is a fairly standard recommendation. This number applies to pure IP environments. Most environments are pure IP (or at least should be by now) but if your network is running a mixed protocol environment, the max size for single flat switched network is smaller, around 100-150 devices per VLAN is recommended. This is because if you run multiple protocols on devices and servers the service advertisement for those devices increases as you add each additional protocol.

Broadcasts and Your Network

In the early days of Ethernet networking we worried a lot about minimizing broadcast traffic. This was primarily because we only had half-duplex, 10Mbps networks. In short, bandwidth was limited. All these years later we're running 1Gbps networks as an industry and 10Gbps is just around the corner. Broadcasts tend to be very small packets and the traffic very bursty in nature. As an industry, we don't worry much anymore about broadcasts eating up tons of bandwidth because even in a broadcast intensive environment, we have so much available bandwidth that the impact of those small broadcast packets is usually negligible. Furthermore, contemporary switches have many features to limit or eliminate networking loops and broadcast storms. Spanning tree protocol is an example of one such feature.

PCs and servers tend to be quite chatty even when sitting idle. These devices advertise their services via broadcast packets. Switches forward directed traffic to and through discreet ports on the network. In other words, a packet sent to a PC at 192.168.1.200 will go through the network to the switch hosting that device and then, using the MAC address for the device, the switch will send that packet out only one port directly to the PC for which it is intended. Packets with discreet destination addresses aren't flooded across the network anymore as they were in the early days of Ethernet. They are sent directly to the device.

Broadcast packets are different. Broadcast packets are sent to every device on the same VLAN as the sending device. This is because the switches learn the locations of devices from the source MAC address of the sending devices and a broadcast address is never listed as a source address, only a destination. The switch therefore floods the broadcast traffic out of all ports on the VLAN. This means if I have a print server on a VLAN with 200 devices and it advertises its services every 30 seconds via broadcasts, the other 199 devices all receive that broadcast packet.

Now imagine the previously described scenario of a VLAN with 200 devices. Let's say that each of those 200 devices has only a single service it advertises and they all do it once every 30 seconds. This means each device will receive 398 broadcast packets every minute!! The total is only 398 because the sending device does not receive its own broadcasts.

The Million-dollar Secret

Here is why we care: Every time a packet hits a network card in an Intel architecture device, it triggers an interrupt and stops the processor! In the pre-plug-n-play days of our industry we used to have to select interrupts (IRQs) for devices manually through the use of jumpers and dip switches. For many years now "plug-n-pray," er, I mean "plug-n-play" makes this selection for us. But devices like NICs still need an interrupt. Here's how mine looks on the PC where I'm writing this book:

You can see that my NIC is using interrupt 17. An interrupt does just that, it interrupts!! What does it interrupt? A Processor.

So, if you have excessive broadcasts on your network, and especially if those broadcast packets are hitting critical, Intel-architecture devices (like your ESX servers) the servers can experience massive slowdowns as the processor stops to process broadcast packets, most of which the server undoubtedly doesn't need! This means instead of spending CPU cycles on important things, like processing production workloads, your servers may be wasting lots of time being constantly interrupted from completing their work.

A Non-technical Allegory from Daily Life

Have you ever come into the office and had a determination to get a certain amount of work done? Perhaps you have an important project you'd like to complete or some reports you need to get done. You sit down at your desk early in the morning with raw determination to get this specific task done. 5 minutes into the process a co-worker stops buy to say "hi." You spend several minutes with the co-worker, not wanting to be rude, and get back to your work a few minutes later. Shortly thereafter the phone rings. You look at the caller ID and decide to let it go to voice mail. Even though you didn't answer it however, it still interrupted you. You attempt to resume your train of thought and get back to work.

After a while the phone rings again. It's your department head…better answer this one because he knows you're here. You spend a while on that conversation. Just as you're about to get off of the phone a helpdesk call comes in that the internet is down. You get up and begin troubleshooting that problem. You figure out that the WAN line is indeed down and you spend a couple of hours working with your ISP to resolve the problem.

When that's done you realize you're really hungry and a little tired. You look at the clock and it's 12:30…better get some lunch. You come back from lunch and sit down at your desk, attempting to figure out where you were on your reports before you were interrupted. That alone takes 10 minutes. 45 minutes later you realize you need to take a bio break. Besides, you're getting a little sleepy from the post-lunch sugar crash and walking around a bit would help wake you up. Sitting back down at your desk later you make a bit of progress on the reports when the head of the engineering department walks in and needs to discuss procuring some new servers for a special project. He stresses that this is important and want to know if you can speak to their application vendor for him to find out what sort of hardware they need.

The next thing you know, it's 5pm and you've added only a few paragraphs to your reports. You were interrupted so much during the day that your primary tasking suffered at the hands of all of the other intrusions into your day. Can you tell I've been in this industry for a while?

While the analogy doesn't perfectly map it's pretty close. Unnecessary broadcast traffic, especially if excessive, can crush the performance of every server and PC in your environment – at least the ones that use interrupts.

A Real-life Example from a Customer in Nashville

I was in Tennessee a few years back doing a virtualization jump-start engagement. The server team leader, his team and I piled into a conference room and began the weeks work. The customer had a laptop with PowerPoint on it. When he would press the space bar to advance the slides it would take 20-45 seconds to advance to the next slide. If you've ever used PowerPoint you know that slide advancement is pretty much instantaneous.

I looked up at the small switch in the conference room and I noticed that the lights for all ports were blinking like crazy, mostly in unison. Remember switches send directed traffic to individual ports. They send broadcast traffic to all ports on the same VLAN. When you see a switch and the traffic lights are blinking in non-unison you're seeing the effects of directed traffic. Lots of lights flashing all at the same time indicate broadcast (or possibly multicast) traffic. While this isn't a scientific indicator of how much it does pay to observe here. I noticed that his switch traffic lights looked like the muzzles of 24 machine guns all firing in unison…constantly. This caught my attention. I combined that observation with the fact that his laptop was advancing slides really slowly. As the morning continued I found out they had a lot of network performance issues they couldn't explain. Lastly we tried to do a P2V conversion to an ESX server and it failed about 60% through inexplicably.

I asked the customer to do me a favor.

"Before you advance the next PowerPoint slide, please unplug your network cable and let the PC sit for about 30 seconds," I requested. The customer did this as I asked.

"Now press the space bar an advance the slides," I said. The customer did so and the slide transition was instantaneous, exactly what one would expect from a PowerPoint presentation. He kept hitting the space bar over and over in disbelief. It seemed I had magically given his PC a speed boost simply by unplugging the network cable.

At that point in my career I was doing quite a bit of protocol analysis and network design. I happened to have a protocol analyzer on my laptop (pretty power-geeky I know…where's my propeller beanie). I asked the customer if I could do a 5 minute capture of network traffic. He said I could.

We found out with a simple 5 minute capture that this customer was averaging around 290 broadcasts per second on his network. I began to ask some questions about the environment and I knew the questions to ask. I found out that this organization had about 500 devices on a single, flat, switched VLAN. These devices included around 300+ user PCs and 50+ servers. Interestingly about 60% of the broadcast traffic was coming from a single device…their VOIP PBX.

I explained that the reason his PC was so slow was that it was getting crushed, machine-gun-style, by lots of annoying broadcast packets which were interrupting (read stopping) the processor around 290 times per second on average!! Not only was this so but every other Intel PC and server on their network was also suffering from the same amount of abuse.

I seriously thought this guy was going to cry. They had major performance problems for a couple of years and consultants and new hardware had been unable to figure out why.

One additional note on this: This particular client had a router/switch-proficient employee who for years said the network had nothing to do with the problem. The reason he came to this conclusion was all of the ports on his switches, network wide, showed relatively low levels of utilization. Again, rare is the PC or server these days that will max out a gigabit NIC. The reason for this is that the broadcast packets are very small and even though there were a lot of them, they came nowhere near having a major impact on total bandwidth consumption. If you happened not to know this little factoid regarding interrupts, NICs and broadcasts you could easily look right past the problem and never see it.

The good news is this is an easy problem to fix. You simply logically divide the network into separate VLANs. This decreases the size of the broadcast domains and radically reduces the impact of those protocols. I showed the customer how to do this with no down time and no need to change the IP on the servers because changing the IPs on 50+ servers would be a real pain.

Customer happy. Problem solved. With this in mind, let's review How NOT To – Item #5 for this chapter: Please do not have large, flat, switched VLANs that far exceed industry recommended sizes so the broadcasts of everything affect everything else on the network.

How NOT to properly setup your virtual networking
Avoid using strict access lists to keep user traffic off of management VLANs

Of course from a security perspective tossing all of this server, management and storage traffic into a single network is a nightmare as well. It's safe to assume that your users have access to your server IP subnets for day-to-day work. If the management and storage pieces are on the same subnets as your server VMs, your users likely have access to those critical devices as well. Users should never be able to access storage and management IPs directly. According to industry studies around 80% of all network misuse is the result of employees either playing around or outright hacking on the corporate network. Even if you don't have problems with employees misusing the network (most companies do and don't know about it) users having access to critical storage and management subnets can provide convenient access to such components for viruses and external intruders.

I've seen a number of viruses over the years that will inspect the infected machines IP address and then begin spreading themselves, PC to PC, server to server around the network simply by scanning for other IP devices on those subnets and spreading around the network. One virus I saw in Florida a number of years ago spread through an entire subnet in under an hour.

Having separate VLANs for management IPs such as ESX Service Console NICS and iSCSI and NAS storage devices not only protects these critical pieces of infrastructure from overbearing broadcast traffic, it also allows us to use access lists to restrict access to them.

A user should never need direct access to your IP storage device. Neither should user subnets need access, in almost all cases, to the Service Console NICs of your ESX servers. So, simple access lists preventing all user subnets from accessing management-device-subnets and storage subnets is an easy, and fairly bullet-proof method for protecting these critical devices. If I have such protection in place, even if a user gets a virus, intruder or malware that is scanning for access to other devices, they simply won't be able to get there because of the access lists.

This in mind let's review How Not to Item number 6 for this chapter: Please do NOT avoid using strict access lists to keep user traffic off of management and storage VLANs.

How TO properly setup your virtual networking
1. Determine Relative Utilization
2. Follow VMware best practices: Shared Virtual Switches and Dedicated Virtual Switches
3. Isolate storage and management traffic (Service Console/VMotion™) from user/server traffic and storage traffic
4. Make sure you have no more than 300 devices in a single, pure IP VLAN. No more that 100-150 devices in a mixed protocol environment
5. Use access lists to keep users from accidently or intentionally connecting to anything in the Storage IP network

How TO properly setup your virtual networking
Determine Relative Utilization

Determine which VMs are low network I/O utilization and which, relative to most, have high Network I/O requirements. This step is absolutely necessary for following VMware's best practices for virtual switch design. Stated another way, it is impossible for you to follow virtual switch configuration best practices if you do not know the relative utilization of your virtual machines.

Follow VMware Best Practices: Shared Virtual Switches and Dedicated Virtual Switches

Shared Virtual Switches – In this scenario we build a virtual switch, connect it to at least two physical NICs for load-balancing and failover. Then we connect multiple relatively low network I/O VMs to this virtual switch. These will use the default load balance which means the VMs will each be assigned to particular NICs by the ESX server.

With this methodology, be sure to monitor utilization on the physical NICs connected to the virtual switch. As you add VMs to this shared virtual switch, make sure you're not maxing-out available bandwidth on any of the NICs. The easiest way to do this is to connect to the management interface of your switch (assuming you have a manageable switch) and look at averages and spikes for port activity on the ports connected to the NICs used by this virtual switch.

Dedicated Virtual Switches – This methodology we build a virtual switch, connect it to multiple physical NICs and connect high network I/O VMs to this virtual switch. We can also use this method for IP storage since a) IP storage should have as much available bandwidth as possible and b) It's a good idea to isolate IP based storage to its own VLAN anyway.

You may want to dedicate an entire virtual switch to a single application in this scenario if its bandwidth utilization justifies an entire 1GB NIC, even if only during spikes in activity. Remember, the default ESX load balance is a round-robin approach to load balancing wherein VMs are pinned to an individual NIC. So if I take a very busy Email server VM and connect it to a dedicated virtual switch which is connected to two physical NICs, the Email VM will still only use one of the NICs. The other will be there for standby. Therefore, if you want to use the throughput of both NICs you can enable link aggregation for the vSwitch in vCenter. Note that your physical switch must support link aggregation and be configured accordingly for the ports connecting to the NICs in this virtual switch.

Let's take a look at how this might look in production:

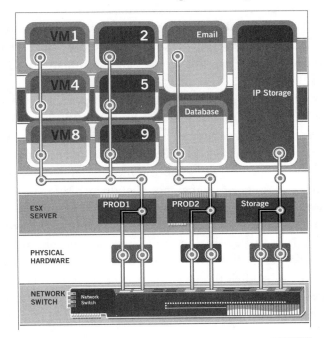

Shared Virtual Switch - PROD1
(default load balance)

VM1	-	Low Network I/O
VM2	-	Low Network I/O
VM4	-	Low Network I/O
VM5	-	Low Network I/O
VM8	-	Low Network I/O
VM9	-	Low Network I/O

Dedicated Virtual Switch - PROD2
(Link Aggregation)

Email	-	High Network I/O
Database	-	High Network I/O

Adaptive Scheme - STORAGE
(Link Aggregation)

IP STORAGE	-	High Network I/O
	-	Separate VLAN
	-	Isolated for security
	-	Isolated from broadcasts
	-	Use access lists to limit access

Here we see that VMs 1,2,4,5,8,9 were found to have relatively low network utilization and we could therefore toss the VMs on the same vSwitch. The Email server and Database server were found to have, relative to the normal, generic VMs, much higher network I/O needs and therefore were given a dedicated vSwitch with two NICs and link aggregation setup on the NICs and physical switch. IP Storage was given its own NICs and placed on its own VLAN to isolate it from broadcast traffic. We should also use access lists to limit access to this network. I recommend only allowing traffic from the networks of servers that will use this storage and administrator IP addresses.

Note that none of this configuration is possible unless we complete step 1, which is to determine relative utilization. For small environments where you feel relatively sure bandwidth is never going to be an issue, feel free to place all of the VMs on shared vSwitches, do some monitoring, and then, if you find that you do need to give more bandwidth to certain VMs you can always easily create new virtual switches and move the VMs to those new virtual switches. Reconfiguring IP storage however, is not so easily done and I recommend placing it on an isolated VLAN from the beginning. Granted, in a very small environment bandwidth may never be an issue, but isolating the storage from other traffic, users and potentially harmful software (like a virus that scans IPs on a given subnet) is always a good idea.

Isolate storage and management traffic (Service Console/ VMotion™vMotion™) from user/server traffic and storage traffic.

Adding a vSwitch to your virtual environment that is dedicated to Service Console and VMotion™ is a good idea as well. The Service Console NIC provides console access to VMs, HA/ DRS communications and other items. It is common to see VMotion™ traffic share this network/NICs as well.

In implementing these first 3 steps you should end up with the following:

- Shared vSwitches hosting generic, low network I/O VMs
- Dedicated vSwitches hosting one or a small number of high network I/O VMs, possibly using link aggregation

- vSwitch for management traffic
- vSwitch for Storage

If you consider that we need at least 2 NICs per virtual switch for failover, this means you will need 8 NICs per ESX server.

Of course for very small shops with a handful of VMs, you could place all of this on a single virtual switch with a few NICs attached to it and "get away with it." As the environment type grows however, the first thing that should be moved to its own NICs is storage, followed by management functionality. Check your switch statistics to determine utilization levels. As is always the case with these things use your best judgment given the environmental needs

Make sure you have no more than 300 devices in a single, pure IP VLAN. No more that 100-150 devices in a mixed protocol environment.

The idea here is to reduce the size of broadcast domains thereby reducing the number of broadcasts/second hitting NICs and interrupting processors. With this we're not really concerned with bandwidth utilization or the ability of the network to handle these broadcasts. We're concerned with stopping broadcasts from beating up on processors. Also keep in mind, these are maximums.

Use access lists to keep users from accidently or intentionally connecting to anything in the Storage IP network

Summary

As with all things virtual, understanding best practices and why/how they are applied allows us to configure our environment in a way that is logical and should provide predictable, stable performance. Following the steps outlined in this chapter will allow you to configure your ESX networking environment efficiently and in keeping with best practices.

How TO properly setup your virtual networking

1. Determine Relative Utilization
2. Follow VMware best practices: Shared and Dedicated Virtual Switches
3. Isolate storage and management traffic (Service Console/ vMotion™) from user/server traffic and storage traffic

4. Make sure you have no more than 300 devices in a single, pure IP VLAN. No more that 100-150 devices in a mixed protocol environment
5. Use access lists to keep users from accidently or intentionally connecting to anything in the Storage IP network

Chapter 5

Memory for Virtual Environments

How NOT to properly manage memory in a virtual environment

1. Pay no attention to memory allocation allowing some ESX servers to become overcommitted for RAM while others lie underutilized.
2. Make no attempt to maintain like VMs thereby decreasing the amount of shared RAM in your environment.
3. Assign RAM to VMs without any post-build investigation to determine if RAM assignments are too high, too low, or about right.
4. Allow restrictive limits to be assigned to "golden masters" which will then be propagated to production VMs through templating and cloning, thus restricting RAM availability to these VMs, guaranteeing poor performance.
5. Pay no attention to balloon driver inflation and deflation
6. Allow VMkernel swap to be used in your production environment

Chapter Introduction

In this chapter we will take a look at memory management for ESX servers. Like the previous chapters, we must understand some basic principles of how ESX uses RAM so we can understand how to screw it up or how NOT to do it correctly. Then we'll take a look at how to properly utilize RAM in your ESX server environment in order to improve performance of the servers and ROI for our investment in virtualization. As always we'll toss in some real-world examples.

How Memory in ESX server Works

Every ESX server has a certain amount of RAM installed in the physical server. ESX server, at this point in time, really contains two operating systems. An ESX server contains a small lightly-modified version of Redhat Linux called the Service Console. This small OS is loaded into the lowest RAM pages available in the server. ESX server also has the VMKernel. This is loaded in the upper pages of RAM in the ESX server.

VMware has also released a version of ESX server known as ESXi (the "I" stands for embedded). In this version of ESX server there is no service console and the Kernel can be run from NVRAM in the server. VMware has made it publically known that at some point in the not-to-distant future they will be moving away from the traditional ESX architecture which has a Service Console and will rely totally on the imbedded technology. Today however, legacy ESX is by far and away the majority of ESX server installations so we will focus on that version here.

So, the RAM layout in an ESX server looks like the illustration below:

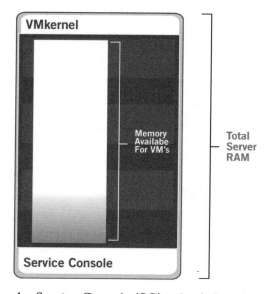

Notice that the Service Console (SC) is loaded in the lowest portion of RAM and the VMKernel is loaded in the highest pages of RAM. The memory between these two is what is left available for Virtual Machines. One thing that changes when you virtualize is that we tend to purchase servers that contain much more RAM and network interface cards (NICs). The reason for this is that before virtualization, we ran a single operating system (OS) on each box. After virtualization we can run many OS's on each physical server. ESX servers running 20-40 virtual machines are not uncommon. All of those operating systems and application need lots of RAM. Don't worry however, as we'll see in a few minutes ESX is very efficient in the way it uses RAM.

Service Console RAM

By default the Service Console receives very little RAM in the ESX server. Numerous management functions and some applications utilize the Service Console to verying degrees. For example, when you use the

VI Client and remote console into a VM, this activity uses the service console. Also, many backup and replication technologies can use the service console. Increasing SC RAM to its maximum can help these functions perform better.

TECH TIP: The maximum memory you can assign to the Service Console is 800MB. It's a good idea to increase Service Console RAM to 800MB at the time of ESX server install. You can modify this setting after installation but your SC swap file will be undersized. When you install ESX server the server sets the SC swap file size to 2x SC RAM. If you go with a default RAM setting at installation (let's say 272MB) ESX will make swap 2x272MB or 544MB. If you later increase SC RAM to 800MB the swap will not be adjusted to 1.6GB so it's best to make this setting up front.

VMKernel RAM Utilization

The VMKernel uses a very small amount of RAM in the highest RAM pages in the server. It uses RAM for itself and also a few kb of management RAM for each virtual machine actively running in the ESX server. As you increase the number of VMs running on any ESX server, careful attention will reveal that the amount of RAM in use by the VMKernel will increase as the number of running VMs goes up. Don't worry however, the amount of RAM used for VM management is very small.

Virtual Machine RAM Utilization

Let's review our RAM layout diagram:

As a simple example let's assume we have a server with 8GB of RAM installed. We set Service Console RAM to 800MB at the time of install, in keeping with best practices, and the VMKernel uses a small amount of additional RAM which will vary slightly according to the number of VMs running on the ESX server. For our example let's assume, as indicated in the picture above, that we have around 7GB of RAM available in the server. This is the RAM in which we run VMs.

ESX server will map pages of VM RAM to separate pages of RAM in the ESX server. For example imagine we have 5 VMs configured as follows:

VM1	-	2GB RAM
VM2	-	1GB RAM
VM3	-	1GB RAM
VM4	-	512MB RAM
VM5	-	2GB RAM

If you add all of those RAM requirements up you'll see that these VMs need a total of 6.5GB of RAM. Conveniently this fits within the amount of RAM we have available in the ESX server.

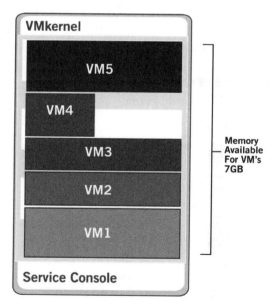

Here we can see, theoretically, that each VM has its memory mapped to a certain place in ESX server memory. The VMKernel, of course, manages all of this. We must understand a few more features and terms of ESX server memory management before we can understand how NOT to properly manage ESX server memory.

Shared RAM

In our example scenario above, imagine if all of those VMs were running the same OS and patch revision, Windows 2003 server with the most recent patches, for example. If that were the case it makes sense that many items in RAM in the various virtual machines would be exactly alike. We would have .exe files, .com files and other parts of Windows, for example, that would be identical and loaded into RAM in each virtual machine.

ESX has the ability to scan RAM pages of the virtual machines and identify duplicate pages. It will then use a single location in RAM for those duplicate pages and "point" multiple virtual machines to that single page of shared RAM. This shared RAM location is flagged read-only(RO) so it stays consistent among the VMs sharing it. The VMs, of course, are completely unaware of this RAM sharing. Each VM simply knows that it has certain information located in a given page of RAM.

Let's imagine we have 10 VMs sharing a certain page of memory and suddenly one of the VMs changes the information in the page of its own memory. What does ESX do? It writes a separate read-write(RW) page of physical RAM for that VM and allows that VM to reference the adjusted page. The other 9 VMs continue running off of the shared RAM page as long as they continue to use that common data.

ESX server is always working toward optimization. Shared RAM allows ESX server to use less physical RAM than would otherwise be needed to accommodate a set of VMs.

TECH TIP: Shared RAM is a great optimization feature but it's important to note that when you first boot an ESX server and load VMs into memory the VMs each get their own isolated memory space. There is no RAM sharing initially because ESX server has not had time to go through the RAM pages of the VMs, identify the duplicate information and create shared pages yet.

It's not uncommon to see ESX servers with 30% of their used RAM acting as shared RAM if the VMs are running like OS's. There's a hint there on a best practice which we'll review later.

Memory Over-commitment

ESX servers can be over-committed for memory. This means you can assign more RAM to VMs than physically exists in the ESX server. In our example above we have 7GB of RAM available for virtual machines. We could actually build VMs with RAM requirements in excess of the 7GB physically available and ESX has mechanisms for dealing with this. Notice I didn't say that we should over-commit our ESX servers, but we can. Let's review the mechanisms available for dealing with RAM crises in ESX server.

The Memory Control Driver (AKA: "Balloon Driver")

When you install the VMware Tools into a virtual machine a memory control driver (vmmemctl) is installed as part of these tools. This driver is used by ESX server to force VMs to give up some of their RAM and begin using their own swap file. Why would ESX do this? If there is more demand for RAM than actually exists in the ESX server. The balloon driver is "inflated" and the VMs are forced to move some contents of their own RAM into the guest OS swap file within their own virtual disks. OF course when this happens the VM will no function in a degraded state of performance because swapping always performs more poorly than using RAM. RAM access is faster than hard disk access.

This begs the question, if I have 20 VMs on an ESX server and the server is overcommitted for RAM, which VMs are forced to give up memory and begin using swap? ESX server chooses the VMs that are to give up RAM based upon proportional shares.

Each virtual machine is assigned shares for RAM usage. These shares are only used in contention. In other words the shares sit there unused unless there is a crisis and a decision must be made by ESX server regarding which VMs get priority access to RAM. By default each VM gets 10 shares per megabyte of assigned RAM.

This means that a VM with 1024MB of RAM will have 10240 shares and a VM with 512MB of RAM will have 5120 shares. If a shortage of memory occurs in the ESX server, ESX uses the shares to determine which VM should give up some RAM. Guess which VM "loses" (and is forced to give up RAM)? The VM with the lesser amount of shares "loses" the share comparison and is forced to give up RAM. The assumption is that RAM is a more critical resource for a VM with a greater assignment of RAM. In other words, a DHCP VM with 1024MB of RAM presumably needs RAM less critically than a Database VM with 8192MB of RAM assigned to it. In this example the DHCP VM will have 10240 shares of RAM while the Database VM has 81920 shares. In a crisis, the DHCP VM will be forced to give up RAM via balloon driver activity first. This sounds pretty logical to me don't you think?

So, the balloon driver inflates when VMs need to give up some RAM and once the crisis is over, the balloon driver should deflate, thus allowing the VM to resume using RAM and allowing it to stop using its own swap file as much, thus improving performance. All of this in mind, it should be obvious that the memory control driver is a nice safety feature to keep ESX from crashing in a memory crisis. It should also be obvious that since there is always a performance degradation of some degree whenever we use swap, that we should avoid deliberate use of balloon driver and memory over-commitment of ESX server.

VMKernel Swap

After building a virtual machine, the first time the VM is powered on a VMKernel swap file is created for the VM in the folder on the VMFS volume that contains the virtual machine. This VMKernel swap file is equal in size to the amount of RAM assigned to the virtual machine.

Here we see the files associated with a virtual machine with the VMKernel swap file highlighted

In a healthy environment, this swap file sits unused. It is just there in case the ESX server needs it in a memory crisis.

If the ESX server is overcommitted for RAM, in other words if there is more demand for RAM by the VMs than physically exists, ESX server will first use the balloon driver to force VMs to give up some of their RAM and begin using their own swap file. If the crisis continues to expand ESX server will begin to grab parts of VM memory and move it out to VMKernel swap. Note that at this point VMs may have double swapping occurring. They may be swapping internally because of balloon driver activity and also have ESX server moving portions of active RAM to disk in the VMKernel swap file. Guess what this can do to your VM performance? It can crush it. A quote from VMware's VI3 VCP training manual says "…use of VMKernel swap is a last resort and performs poorly."

It's a testament to the resilience of ESX server that you can grossly overcommit the server and it can still stay up, along with its VMs, because of these safety features. Ballooning and VMKernel swap are great safety mechanisms that can keep your server from crashing but these features should not be leaned upon for constant use as performance will be degraded to varying degrees when using these features.

Now that we understand the basics of ESX Server memory management, let's take a look at how NOT to properly manage memory in a virtual environment.

How NOT to properly manage memory in an virtual environment

Pay no attention to memory allocation allowing some ESX server to become overcommitted for RAM while others lie underutilized.

I've actually heard of admins advocating deliberately over-committing ESX Server RAM since VMware has all of these optimization and safety features. Features like the memory control driver and VMKernel swap are amazing safety features. Having VMs running in these states however will definitely degrade performance of the VMs so please avoid it.

Before virtualization, whenever we wanted to acquire and set-up a new server, doing so could easily be a multi-week process. We may have to have a bunch of meetings, call the software vendor, spec a server, get price quotes, get budgeting approved, order the server, rack and cable the new server and install the OS and apps along with any other standard pieces of software we use in our environment. Now that we're virtualizing as an industry we have a new problem, "VM sprawl." VM sprawl refers to the endless creation of VMs for every little thing. The reality is that now we can bring a new server (VM) online in a few minutes with templates and clones. As an industry, because we can, we do, and it's very common now to see IT departments building lots of new VMs that they may not need. The perception becomes "VMs are free" since we can create them so easily now. The reality is of course, there are costs associated with each VM we build.

Failure to pay attention to ESX server RAM utilization or worse yet, deliberate over-allocation will lead to sub-optimal and perhaps even poor VM performance in your environment. Failure to leave spare capacity for your HA/DRS clusters, so that VMs can failover to other ESX servers when needed, can take your servers from an over-allocated state to a grossly over-allocated state very quickly.

Make no attempt to maintain like VMs thereby decreasing the amount of shared RAM in your environment.

Remembering our discussion on shared RAM, ESX server looks for duplicate RAM pages and allocates single, RO RAM pages for multiple VMs when it can do so. One way to use RAM inefficiently is to provision lots of completely different VMs on the same ESX server.

If I build my VMs with no internal consistency this means the VMs on each ESX server will have less duplicate pages of RAM and ESX therefore can share fewer pages of physical memory. This increases utilization of memory in the ESX server.

If I have, on a single ESX server, 4 different versions of Windows, a few Linux VMs of various version, perhaps a couple of other OS's and no service pak/patch consistency I lessen the ability of ESX server to find duplicate pages and therefore cause it to use more RAM to host the same number of VMs. Of course aside from ESX server and virtualization this is sloppy IT practice anyway and should be avoided. For our purposes in this chapter, this is definitely an inefficient way to utilize RAM. Having many OS's on the same ESX server also reduces processing performance because the processor caches must constantly be cleared and reloaded in busy environments.

Assign RAM to VMs without any post-build investigation to determine if RAM assignments are too high, too low, or about right.

Whenever we build a VM we are forced to best-guess how much RAM needs to be assigned to the VM. Whenever we chose a RAM assignment for a VM always one of three things is going to happen:

- We guess high and over assign RAM to the VM
- We estimate about right and the VM has an appropriate amount of RAM
- We guess low and the VM is using all of its RAM and probably its own swap file as well, lessening performance.

One of the ways we can poorly manage ESX server RAM is by failing to review our assignments after the fact. VMs that are grossly over-assigned waste RAM. VMs that are under-assigned perform poorly.

Allow restrictive limits to be assigned to "golden masters" which will then be propagated to production VMs through templating and cloning, thus restricting RAM availability to these VMs, guaranteeing poor performance.

In virtual environments we should build base images of the operating systems we use and spawn new VMs from these base images via templates or clones. These base images are referred to in the industry as "golden masters." The golden masters allow us to maintain operational consistency across our virtual machines. These images should contain our standard OS builds, the latest service packs and patches, backup agents, antivirus agents and other software common to the VMs in our organization.

One common mistake that we see in the industry is to have a limit applied to the golden master memory settings. If you right-click on a VM and view its memory settings in vCenter you will see that we can assign maximum RAM to a VM and we can also assign limits and minimum RAM. A VM will never be forced to give up RAM by the balloon driver that causes it to drop below its minimum RAM assignment.

Here we see where one can set a limit on a VM – please don't do this

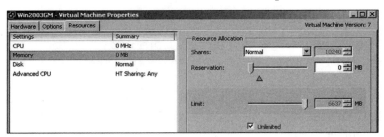

Limits tell ESX server the maximum amount of physical RAM pages to allocate to a VM. The limit always wins. If you've assigned 4GB of RAM to a VM and "accidently" have a limit of 1GB assigned as well, that VM will never receive more than 1GB of physical RAM pages from ESX server. Of course the VM is unaware of this. The VM "thinks" it has 4GB, its guest OS is being told by ESX server that is has 4GB but ESX will never allocate more than the limit, in this example, 1GB. Naturally this will crush VM performance if the VM actually needs the RAM you've assigned to it. There is a great article about how this misconfiguration affects VM performance here: *http:// www.vmguru.com/index.php/articles-mainmenu-62/mgmt-and- monitoring-mainmenu-68/96-memory-behavior-when-vm- limits-are-set.*

For our purposes assigning limits that conflict with VM memory assignments is a great way to NOT properly manage ESX server memory.

If this is such a screw-up, why is it so common? Because sometimes the golden master will have a limit applied. Admins use the golden master to spawn new VMs via golden master templates, unaware that a limit has been assigned to the golden master. The admins are making production RAM assignments to VMs unaware that a limit is applied that will invalidate all of their assignments.

Pay no attention to balloon driver inflation and deflation

Proper memory management of an ESX server, as you can probably tell by now requires proactive performance monitoring to make sure the environment in configured optimally. One great way to improperly manage ESX server memory is to fail to do this performance monitoring, let it run and wish for the best.

Failure to take notice that VMs have inflated balloon drivers and that they are being forced to give up RAM and use swap is a great way to degrade performance of your virtual environment. If balloon drivers are inflated you need to find out why and correct it.

Failure of balloon drivers to deflate is a common problem in the industry. When this happens the VM is being kept in a degraded state of performance unnecessarily. Unless you want to go through all of your VMs on a constant basis looking for these sort of problems, a virtualization aware performance monitoring tool is a must. There are many good ones in the industry. Quest Software's vFoglight Pro finds many of the memory issues described in this chapter.

Some applications don't work well with balloon driver activity. Check with your application vendors (in particular with databases) to find out if there are any known issues. You can disable the balloon driver in VMs where there exist potential conflicts.

Allow VMkernel swap to be used in your production environment

This last problem is another inattention issue. Again, VM memory management is all about paying attention and understanding how it works. Failure to do this results in poor performance.

Obviously failure to notice VMKernel swapping in an environment is going to crush performance. Remember the VMware quote: "…use of VMKernel swap is a last resort and performs poorly." I met a guy in Orlando, Florida while teaching a VCP class there. On a break from class he asked if we could make a Citrix connection back into his network to look at the memory allocation of his ESX servers (this was in the ESX 2 days). We looked at the management interface and found that about 30% of his VMs were using VMKernel swap. He was actually overjoyed. Now that he understood his performance problem he could fix it.

How TO properly manage memory in a virtual environment

Pay close attention to memory allocation of your ESX servers. Always allocate memory in keeping with what is actually available in RAM while maintaining enough spare capacity to allow HA/DRS clusters to perform properly.

Over-commitment of ESX Server RAM can easily happen by creating more and more VMs over time without paying attention to server RAM actually available. It's imperative in a virtual environment to use alarms and monitoring tools that will alert us when our ESX servers and VMs are becoming maxed regarding RAM utilization.

The ability to over-commit an ESX server should be seen/used as a safety/emergency feature. We should always allocate RAM to our VMs in accordance with what RAM is actually available. For HA/DRS clusters, we actually have to leave spare capacity available for the clusters to function properly.

Maintain like VMs (OS/patch revisions/standard corporate applets) as much as reasonably possible thereby increasing duplicate RAM pages and the amount of shared RAM in your environment.

As much as reasonably possible use consistent OS builds in your environment and in particular on each ESX server. Building same OS/patch revision VMs on your ESX servers implicitly creates more duplicate RAM pages. This increases the ability of ESX server to consolidate those RAM pages to Shared RAM space in memory. This allows us to use less physical RAM to accommodate the same number of virtual machines.

Note that designation of shared RAM and consolidation of RAM pages takes time. This does not happen immediately. Therefore, if we boot an ESX server with 20 VMs on it and power on the VMs, the ESX server initially needs to have adequate RAM to accommodate all of these VMs in memory. This reinforces the previous best practice of avoiding deliberate over-allocation of ESX servers. As the ESX server consolidates RAM to Shared RAM pages over time, memory utilization on the ESX server decreases. This allows even more spare capacity to accommodate failover and spikes in activity.

Assign RAM to VMs in accordance with expected workload requirements and review these assignments after the fact, making adjustments where necessary.

As you build virtual machines in your environment its useful to review the RAM assignments you've made. If you find VMs that have been under-assigned RAM, increasing the amount of RAM given to the virtual machines can avoid swap file use and improve VM performance. If you find VMs that are grossly over-assigned RAM reducing these assignments can free-up wasted RAM in your ESX servers.

To review RAM assignments of the VMs in your environment, it is inadequate to simply console into the VM one day and look at how much RAM is being used. You may see a VM that appears to be using far less RAM than is assigned at this moment but that VM may indeed use much more or even all of its assigned RAM during spikes in activity related to authentication cycles (I.e. beginning-of-the-day login time) or business activity/cycles. It is necessary to view VM RAM utilization over time and adjust RAM assignments in a way that accommodates the VMs maximum use of memory. For this, advanced monitoring tools that baseline the environment are a must simply because it's not practical to "keep an eye on it" consistently with many VMs over time.

Make sure your golden masters have no limits applied to them. Moreover, never use limits at all. If you need to reduce RAM allocation to a VM simply reduce the max assignment, don't use a limit.

Limits create a conflict between how much RAM the VM is being told it has by ESX server and what the server will actually allocate. This is not a good idea. Please don't use them. Give the VMs a RAM assignment appropriate for their workloads, review it afterwards using baseline information that includes spikes in activity, avoid limits and let it run.

Pay attention to balloon driver inflation and deflation

If you have ballooning taking place in your VMs find out why and fix it. Perhaps the ESX server is overcommitted. Maybe the ESX server has plenty of RAM but the VM is a member of a resource pool with expandable reservations disabled and a limit is applied to the resource pool. Check to see if the VM itself has a limit applied that it received from a golden master. All of these things can cause balloon driver activity.

If some of your applications have known incompatibilities with balloon drivers, disable the balloon driver in those VMs.

Avoid VMkernel swap to be used in your production environment

If your VMs are using VMkernel swap they probably have 2 instances of swapping going on and are being starved for RAM. Do whatever it takes to eliminate the memory crisis. Solutions include adding more memory to ESX Server, reducing RAM assignments of VMs that are over-assigned, eliminating unnecessary VMs (reducing VM sprawl) or even purchasing new servers.

Summary

Proper memory management in a virtual environment is all about being proactive and aware as well as understanding how the server works. The information in this chapter can help you properly manage ESX Server and VM memory. Unless you want to look through your environment on a constant, repeating basis to find these issues, a virtualization-aware performance monitoring tool is a must. Such applications sit as an expert keeping an "eye" on your environment 24/7 and proper alarms and alert let you know when memory issues arise.

Chapter 6

Managing Processor Use for Virtual Environments

How NOT to properly manage processor in a virtual environment

1. Fail to understand how processor scheduling works in your ESX server. Just toss VMs out there and hope for the best
2. Mix single, dual and quad proc VMs on all of your ESX servers
3. Fail to reduce VMs to single proc VMs leaving many cores scheduled but underutilized
4. Pay no attention to important counters like CPU %Ready
5. Maintain little to no consistency amongst guest OS types, versions and service packs thus reducing speed enhancements provided by processor cache
6. As you P2V physical machines into your environment, just migrate them as they are with no attention to how to do P2V migrations properly

Chapter Introduction

Typically when organizations virtualize their environment, admins begin by virtualizing systems that are relatively non-critical and relatively low utilization. Servers like DHCP, DNS, file & Print and others are usually chosen to be migrated into the virtual environment first. Why? Two reasons:

1. Admins have to build their confidence in ESX server stability
2. Admins have to build their confidence in their own ability to manage the new virtual environment

In short, most admins prefer to "tip-toe" into the virtualization pool rather than dive in head first and hope for the best. This in itself is not a bad practice

After some amount of time goes by, assuming the admins feel comfortable with VMware software and their ability to manage it, we usually begin to migrate more critical systems into the virtual environment. Servers like Exchange, SQL, Sharepoint and many others are often considered for migration into the virtual environment at this point. Very often this is where performance problems begin.

What I have seen happen over and over to various organizations is that they will migrate critical systems into the virtual environment and have problems they can't resolve and that seem to make no sense at all. Often, if the performance issues are bad enough, someone in authority in the organization makes a decision to migrate those systems back to physical servers and then the company will adopt a very conservative posture toward virtualization. I've heard admins and managers make statements like "We don't virtualize critical apps because they don't perform well virtualized."

The reality is there is no need for such a conservative posture toward virtualization. Companies by the thousands virtualize critical apps each year globally. But we do need to have an understanding of how the ESX server works so we can properly troubleshoot and resolve performance issues. This is especially true when it comes to understanding how virtual machines are scheduled to processor resources. I meet people all of the time who think virtual machines on an ESX server are all running at the same time on processor, a kind of ESX server super-computing. This however, is not how virtual machines get access to processor. In an ESX server virtual machines are scheduled to processor by the kernel. This implicitly means there are times they are not scheduled to a processor.

For a detailed technical description of how ESX Server schedules VMs to processor please read the following document http://www.vmware.com/files/pdf/perf-vsphere-cpu_scheduler.pdf . Also, all good ESX admins need to read the ESX Server Resource Management Guide found here http://www.vmware.com/pdf/vsphere4/r40/vsp_40_resource_mgmt.pdf . For my part, I'm going to take a "plain language" approach to explaining how ESX server schedules VMs to processor in this chapter. I don't want readers to get bogged down in technical minutiae and miss the concepts and principles involved. Also, initially I'm going to make general statements about processor scheduling on ESX server and then discuss some performance modifiers for vSphere. vSphere's performance modifiers definitely make scheduling VMs to processor more efficient but we should never design systems around performance modifiers. For system design we should keep in mind the primary principles and allow the performance modifiers to do what they are supposed to do, increase performance a bit.

One quick note: In this chapter pCPU refers to a physical processor/core. vCPU refers to a virtual processor within a VM. If I build a virtual machine and assign it 4 processors in vCenter this means the VM has 4 vCPUs. With that, let's dive into ESX Server processor management.

ESX Server Processor Management – Foundational Elements

Imagine a typical dual-socket, dual-core ESX server. The box has a total of four cores or processors. Now imagine we have 20 VMs on that server. Even if all of the VMs are single vCPU VMs, we still have demand for 20 cores but we only have four in the server. Understanding how ESX provides processor access to all of these VMs is key to managing a virtual environment and the focus of this chapter.

Let's define some general rules for how ESX schedules VMs to processor. These rules used to be strictly applied in ESX version 2 and ESX 3. vSphere (ESX 4) includes performance enhancers that allow them to avoid strict adherence to these rules… a little. We will discuss the performance enhancers after the basic rules are discussed. These rules should still be used for system design and management however.

1. ESX server schedules VMs onto and off-of processor as needed.
2. Whenever a VM is scheduled to processor, all of the cores must be available for the VM to be scheduled or the VM cannot be scheduled at all.
3. If a VM cannot be scheduled to processor when it needs access to processor, VM performance can suffer tremendously.
4. When VMs are "ready" for a processor but unable to be scheduled, this creates what VMware calls "CPU %Ready" values.
5. CPU %Ready manifests as a utilization issue but is actually a scheduling issue.

ESX Server Schedules VMs Onto and Off-of Processor on Demand

In the example scenario mentioned above, I have 4 cores and demand for 20 cores. How does ESX server handle this? It schedules VMs onto and off-of processor as needed very quickly. It's been said a picture is worth 1000 words. That being the case, let's use some illustrations.

Figure A. Dual socket, dual core server with 4 cores available for scheduling

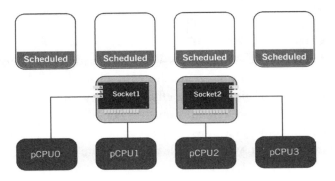

In Figure A we see our aforementioned example scenario depicted (minus the VMs). We have a dual socket, dual core ESX server which of course gives us 4 cores. I am aware that most contemporary servers are at least quad core, but using a fewer number of processors makes it easier to illustrate these points.

Let's collapse the diagram to get rid of the sockets since we don't schedule VMs to sockets, we schedule them to cores. This will simplify our example.

Figure B. Four cores available for scheduling

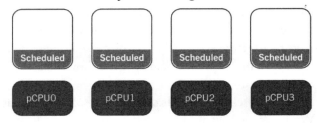

Now let's add some VMs of varying vCPU configuration and see how this scheduling stuff works.

Figure C. Many single vCPU VMs being scheduled to processor in ESX Server

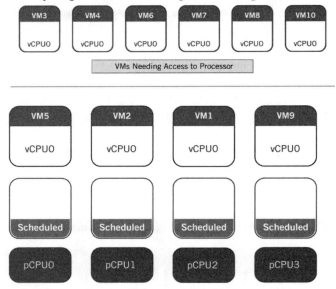

Notice in Figure C. that various VMs are scheduled to processor in this environment. Also notice that because all of the VMs are single vCPU scheduling should be quite efficient. Everytime a VM is moved off of a core a single core is made available. Now ESX server can schedule another VM onto that previously occupied core. This becomes a bit more interesting when we mix single and dual core VMs.

Figure D. Dual-core VM cannot be scheduled because only 1 core is available

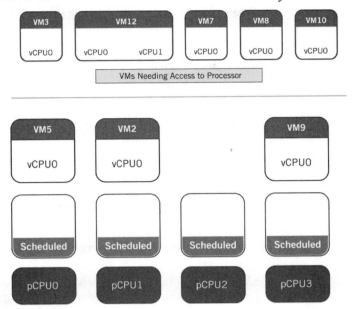

Notice in Figure D. that even though a pCPU is available and VM12 needs access to processor, VM12 cannot be scheduled because only a single core is available. VM12 can exist in a state where it is ready for a processor but cannot get access to one because not enough cores are available for it to be scheduled. Remember (this is important and that's why I'll repeat it several times) this situation creates what VMware calls CPU %Ready values. The VM is "ready" for a processor, but cannot be scheduled to one because adequate cores are not available.

Now let's see what happens we mix single, dual and quad vCPU VMs. *Figure E.*

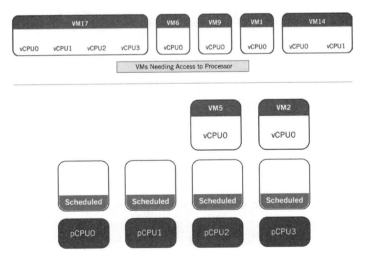

Notice in Figure E. that ESX has 2 cores available. We could schedule VMs 1,6,9, or 14 because they are all single or dual vCPU VMs and we have adequate cores to accommodate their workload. Note however, that VM 17 cannot be scheduled since it has 4 cores and we do not have that many available for scheduling. Perhaps a few milliseconds later ESX has scheduled a dual and a single vCPU VM to processor because adequate cores were available for those VMs. All the while VM17 cannot be scheduled because 4 cores must be available simultaneously. This VM will incur CPU %Ready values in such situations.

To summarize this part of the chapter consider the following:

1. Mixing single, dual and quad vCPU VMs on the same ESX server can create major scheduling problems. This is especially true when the ESX server has low core densities (as in the situation above) and/or when ESX servers average moderate to high utilization levels.

2. Best Practice: Wherever possible reduce VMs to single vCPU VMs. This should include the majority of VMs in almost any environment. There are two exceptions to this rule, 1) If the VM hosts an application that requires multiple processors as recommended by the vendor, 2) When you do the "megahertz-math" and you find you cannot consolidate the workload of a VM onto a single core. For example, if a VM has 2 vCPUs, each averaging around 60% utilization, you cannot collapse that workload onto a single core.

3. Keep an eye on CPU %Ready Values. Keep them at or as close to zero as possible. More than 2% indicates performance\ scheduling issues.

The basic premises of CPU scheduling as stated in the first part of this chapter are strictly adhered to by ESX 2. In VI3 (ESX3) and vSphere (ESX4) VMware introduced some performance enhancers that we will review here. Your virtual environment, however, should not be designed around performance enhancers. The concepts listed above should be the primary consideration when designing and managing your virtual environment. Let's take a look at the performance enhancers in vSphere.

Performance Enhancers for vSphere

Non-scheduling of idle processors – vSphere has the ability to skip scheduling of idle processors. For example if a quad proc VM has activity on only 1 core, vSphere has the ability to schedule only that single core sometimes. Keep in mind that a multi threaded app in a VM will likely be using most or all or it's cores most of the time. If a VM has vCPUs that are sitting idle a lot, it should be reviewed whether or not this VM actually contains a multithreaded app and/or actually needs multiple cores. As most of you realize, if your application isn't multithreaded you gain nothing by assigning multiple cores to the VM and you make the VM more difficult to schedule.

Processor Skew – Guest OSs expect to see progress on all of their cores all of the time. vSphere has the ability to allow a small amount (we're talking milliseconds here) of skew whereby the processors need not be completely in sync. The amount of skew has to be kept within acceptable, small limits in the ESX server.

These are a couple of examples of performance enhancers in vSphere but again, one wouldn't want to design a system based upon these. These simply allow vSphere to perform better than it would lacking these measures.

Cache Problems

Another issue is that vSphere attempts to schedule VMs on the same core over and over again. Imagine we have a Linux OS that has been running for some time on a certain core. Suddenly, for whatever reason, the Linux VM is having scheduling issues and must be moved to another processor. Processor caches contain certain information that allow the OS to perform better. If the VM is moved to a new core on a new socket and the cache isn't shared (it usually isn't across sockets) the cache for this new core must be loaded with the information previously cached on the old processor. If performance losses that will be incurred by moving a VM to a new cache are less than current scheduling delays and inefficiencies, ESX server will move the VM to a new core but this isn't an ideal way to fly.

Once again this is not an attempt to wax to deeply into technical minutia. You can get more than all the technical detail you want out of the documents I listed in the beginning of this chapter. My goal here is to give you plan language concepts so you can understand "the should" and "should-nots" of this chapter. Let's take a look now at a real life example. I've seen processor scheduling issues in many settings. The example I'll provide is taken from a client (that I'll call Company A) which I worked with a few years ago.

Real-world Example with Company A

Company A began virtualizing like many companies do, cautiously. Of course they'd heard all of the hype surrounding virtualization – improved disaster recovery, server consolidation, moving VMs on-the-fly with vVMotion™, etc. Still, they needed to learn to manage VMware and they also needed to see for themselves that it would be stable in their environment. After a number of months the admins in Company A decided to virtualize a few SQL servers. They P2V-migrated these servers into the virtual environment.

Right away they had issues. The helpdesk phone was ringing and users were complaining of poor performance for the apps utilizing these servers. The admins began their troubleshooting by remote consoling into the VMs via the VI Client. The VMs were quite sluggish. If they looked at task manager inside of the guest OS it reported processor utilization at or close to 100%. What was strange however, is that the ESX servers were nowhere near 100% utilization on their cores. True, they were averaging around 50-60% utilization, which is nice, moderate utilization, but there was still plenty of "horse power" for these VMs available. Equally strange was that vCenter reported no errors and the VMs were not maxed in their RAM utilization.

So here we have VMs saying they are maxed for processor, the ESX servers and vCenter look fine with no errors and the helpdesk phone is ringing off the hook. This is the sort of stuff that makes virtual admins' heads spin. Note: Oftentimes when someone is in this sort of situation for a number of days or weeks someone in authority somewhere will make the decision that there will be no more virtualizing critical apps. I've see this happen numerous times.

Fortunately an acquaintance of mine happened to be onsite. He installed a VMware performance monitoring tool with which I was familiar, sent me an email, and asked if I would take a look at this customer's issue. I connected with the customer via a webex meeting, looked around his environment and had the problem solved in 20 minutes (don't we wish they were all that easy). Not only so, but I was able to give the customer simple instructions on how to resolve his issue. Anecdotally the customer purchased 16 sockets of monitoring software less than a week later.

Here is what was happening. When the customer virtualized he Physical-to-virtual (P2V) migrated various VMs as-is into the virtual environment (this is a big no-no that we'll discuss in the chapter on P2V migrations). So if a DHCP server had two processors with 1 running at 1% and the other idle, he would migrate that over, exactly as it was into the virtual environment, which of course meant the new DHCP VM had two processors or two vCPU's. They also built a number of new single and dual vCPU VM's themselves. These SQL VMs were dual and quad core. Consequently he had a big mixture of single dual and quad core VMs running on the same ESX servers. His servers were only dual socket/dual core. This created an ESX scheduling nightmare.

The quad proc VMs (and sometimes the dual-vCPU VMs) would need access to processor but simply couldn't be scheduled efficiently. This client had CPU %Ready values of almost 16% in his VMs. This of course will crush VM performance. The client simply needed to reduce multi-core VMs to single core VM where possible, keep an eye on CPU %Ready to make sure it decreased radically and the problem would be solved. In the case where one has many multi vCPU VMs that actually need to stay multi-vCPU, the best practice is to place them on their own cluster (unless your environment is so large that the scattered multi vCPU VMs create no scheduling issues). CPU %Ready tells you if things are being scheduled efficiently or not.

Imagine an organization with 20 quad vCPU VMs that need to remain quad vCPU. If these VMs are placed in their own cluster, scheduling can be done efficiently. Every time a VM is removed from processor this frees up four cores, which conveniently is exactly the number of cores required to schedule the next VM.

All of this in mind, let's take a look at how NOT to properly manage processor in a virtual environment.

How NOT to properly manage processor in a virtual environment

1. Fail to understand how processor scheduling works in your ESX server. Just toss VMs out there and hope for the best
2. Mix single, dual and quad proc VMs on all of your ESX servers
3. Fail to reduce VMs to single proc VM leaving many cores scheduled but underutilized
4. Pay no attention to important counters like CPU %Ready
5. Maintain little to no consistency amongst guest OS types, versions and service packs thus reducing speed enhancements provided by processor cache
6. As you P2V physical machines into your environment, just migrate them as they are with no attention to how to do P2V migrations properly

Failure to understand how processor scheduling works in your ESX server. Just toss VMs out there and hope for the best.

Hopefully this chapter and others in this book have made it abundantly clear that virtualizing creates an entirely new layer of infrastructure that needs to be properly managed. CPU scheduling and best practices are not difficult to understand and follow. Alternatively, you can toss a bunch of VMs into your environment and hope for the best. Doing so however definitely qualifies for how NOT to properly manage processor in a virtual environment.

I personally speak with thousands of virtualizing organizations every year. I've noted that if I'm speaking in some sort of virtualization forum, a VMware User's Group (VMUG) for example, and I ask for a show of hands in the room regarding how many know what CPU %Ready values are and how they work, I might get 2-5 hands out of 100 people. This is an important counter to understand in your ESX environment.

Mix Single, Dual and Quad Proc VMs on all of your ESX Servers

Since the early days of virtualization this has always been a no-no. Note that this means there shouldn't be any mixture. The higher the core density per server and/or the lower the utilization of the ESX servers, the less impactful this mixture becomes. Environments with 16 cores per server or simply very low utilization can often get away with sever mixture in this area. As soon as moderate utilization levels are reached however, you will likely see CPU% Ready begin to rise. A small amount of mixture (a few multi vCPU VMs in a sea of single proc VMs) may not create any significant delays in scheduling. A heavy mixture however (i.e. 20 VMs on a single server with 8 single vCPU, 6 dual vCPU and 6 quad vCPU will likely be a scheduling catastrophe.

So where is the line then? What ratio of mixture is acceptable? There is no hard definable number. The impact of this phenomena and the rate of occurrence of scheduling issues is all a factor of available cores vs. utilization levels vs. mixture ratio. So as admins we have to understand it, follow best practices and keep an eye on CPU %Ready values.

Fail to Reduce VMs to Single vCPU Leaving Many Cores Scheduled but Underutilized

Assigning multiple vCPUs to VM is only beneficial if the apps running inside of VM are multi-threaded and there is activity on multiple cores. Leaving VMs multi vCPU simply because the systems were that way before they were virtualized is unnecessary and inefficient.

I worked with a client in DC years ago who insisted on building every VM with a corporate standard of at least 4GB of RAM and 2 vCPUs minimum because that was their standard server build before virtualization. Before virtualization such a stance was justifiable because they wanted to make sure that every time they purchased a new physical server it had enough resources to be useful for several years. This paradigm needs to be discarded when creating VMs. When building physical servers we tried to get as much hardware as we could within budget. When building VMs we should be conservative in our assignments, giving the VM just enough resources to carry its workload easily but nothing more. We can always adjust the settings for the VM later if needed.

Pay No Attention to Important Counters Like CPU %Ready

Many admins I meet don't take time to understand the systems they administer at a detailed level. You're reading this book so it's very likely you're not such an admin. Understanding key counters like CPU %Ready is important. In fact, without understanding such counters, it's impossible to troubleshoot performance problems in a virtual environment. Another aspect to this is automated monitoring. We will discuss this in the last chapter.

Maintain little to no consistency amongst guest OS types, versions and service packs thus reducing speed enhancements provided by processor cache

There are many reasons to, as much as possible, maintain like, consistent guest operating systems with same patch revisions, antivirus software, agents, etc. in your environment. Of course such an environment is easier to manage than an environment where the servers have widely scattered OS versions, patch revisions and so on. From a virtualization perspective there are advantages to such uniformity. As we saw in the chapter on proper memory management, like OS's increases ESX server's ability to consolidate RAM pages to Shared RAM pages, thus allowing us to use less RAM for our VMs.

From a processor management perspective, which is what this chapter is all about, there are additional advantages. If my environment is experiencing scheduling issues, it's likely that VMs will be moved around to different cores. Remember, ESX attempts to run VMs on the same core as much as possible. If the scheduling issues outweigh the benefits of running the VMs on the same cores – thus requiring ESX to clear and reload processor caches – then ESX will move the VMs to other cores. Of course this is done at a cost to performance however.

As you P2V physical machines into your environment, just migrate them as they are with no attention to how to do P2V migrations properly

In the P2V chapter we will review P2V best practices and how this is important for maintaining a healthy virtual environment. Failure to follow best practices in this area can bring many problems from your physical environment into your virtual environment. Improperly done P2V migrations can cause VMs to be unstable or crash, fill event logs with useless information and waste resources such as CPU cycles, memory and disk space.

How TO properly manage processor in a virtual environment Determine Relative Utilization

1. Take time to understand and memorize how VMs are scheduled to processor and use this information to quickly troubleshoot your environment when you have CPU or scheduling issues
2. As much as possible avoid extreme mixtures of single, dual and quad proc VMs on the same ESX servers, especially when ESX average utilization levels are above 40%
3. Wherever possible reduce VMs to single VCPU settings remembering the two exceptions and allowing for those

4. Pay attention to CPU %Ready and other critical counters in your environment
5. Maintain consistent guest OS configurations as much as possible
6. Follow P2V best practices and lay a good foundation for your virtual environment

Take time to understand and memorize how VMs are scheduled to processor and use this information to quickly troubleshoot your environment when you have CPU or scheduling issues

Hopefully this chapter has helped provide some insight into how ESX server manages processor utilization. Between this chapter and the two documents linked in the beginning of the chapter you should be well on your way to accomplishing this first objective. This knowledge will make you better equipped to properly manage processor access in your environment and troubleshoot problems in your virtual environment.

As much as possible avoid extreme mixtures of single, dual and quad proc VMs on the same ESX servers, especially when ESX average utilization levels are above 40%

Clearly heavy mixtures of single, dual and quad proc VMs can create scheduling problems in virtual environments. If you do have substantial amounts of multi vCPU VMs, are unable to reduce these VMs to single vCPU and are incurring heavy CPU %Ready values, consider placing these VMs in their own cluster – especially if there are large amounts of quad core VMs.

Wherever possible reduce VMs to single VCPU settings remembering the two exceptions and allowing for those

This is a best practice. Situations in which you can reduce VMs to single vCPU include:

1. The VM consistently has one or more idle processors
2. The VM contains no multithreaded apps
3. The VM's workload can easily be consolidated to a single vCPU

This should include many VMs such as utility servers, DHCP, DNS, File & Print, etc. in many environments. Of course keep in mind the exceptions to this practice:

1. The Guest OS or Application requires multiple CPUs as part of its recommended configuration
2. You do the "megahertz math" and simply find that the workload of the VM cannot be consolidated to a single core.

Pay attention to CPU %Ready and other critical counters in your environment

Virtual environments have numerous critical counters and metrics that are very useful for troubleshooting. Some example include CPU %Ready, VMKernel Swap activity, Shared RAM and others. These indicators and the phenomena they represent didn't exist in the non-virtual world. Taking time to understand what these counters are, what they indicate and where they can be found in vCenter and other performance monitoring tools is paramount to maintaining a health virtual environment.

Maintain consistent guest OS configurations as much as possible

Following this best practice will make your environment easier to manage, increase shared RAM utilization and help maintain strong performance for CPU caching.

Follow P2V best practices and lay a good foundation for your virtual environment

We will review these best practices in the chapter on proper P2V migrations. Following those best practices includes reducing VMs to single vCPU (where possible) as you migrate them into the virtual environment. This of course is part of reducing CPU %Ready and aids in efficient scheduling of VMs to processor.

Summary
CPU scheduling issues often manifest as utilization issues (high apparent utilization) in the Guest OS but really have little to do with utilization. Healthy CPU scheduling can be obtained by following the best

practices outlined in this chapter, thus avoiding the "How NOT To's" of CPU scheduling. Keeping an eye on CPU %Ready in your environment is a good way to be aware of how well ESX scheduling is functioning inside of your servers. CPU %Ready should be kept at or as close to zero as possible. If you have VM2 with 2% CPU %Ready you should find out why. Any VMs with more than 4% are going to have considerable performance degradation. At this level you definitely want to find out what is causing the scheduling delays and take corrective action.

Chapter 7

The Critical Foundation – Proper P2V Migrations

What is a P2V migration? P2V stands for "Physical to Virtual" and a P2V migration refers to the migrating of "physical" – which is to say non-virtual – servers into the virtual environment. The P2V process, under the hood, really has two major phases:

Phase 1 is the imaging of the entire server including the OS, applications and data, into a virtual disk.

Phase 2, which only takes a few seconds, occurs when the physical device drivers are stripped from the OS and replaced with virtual hardware drivers.

When these two phases are complete one has "P2V migrated" a server into the virtual world.

For example, imagine we have a Dell server running a Windows server operating system that we decide to virtualize. In this example, the operating system has device drivers installed for the Dell server and is therefore "bound" to the underlying hardware. Recall that virtualization, by VMware's own definition "…detaches the OS and applications from the underlying hardware…" (VMware VI3 VCP Training Manual). This is done by imaging the server into a virtual machine, stripping out the physical device drivers and replacing them with virtual hardware drivers in the VM as follows.

Phase 1 – Image the Data into a VM

Dell Server
- Windows Server OS bound to hardware by drivers
- Various data and apps totaling 100GB

Dell running ESX Server

Phase 2 – Strip physical hardware drivers out of the guest OS and insert virtual drivers

Dell Server
- Windows Server OS bound to hardware by drivers
- Various data and apps totaling 100GB

Dell running ESX Server

Phase 3 – Shutdown physical server and boot new VM

Dell Server
- Powered Off

Dell running ESX Server
- New VM running Windows
- 100GB of data + free space allocated for growth

There are a number of good applications in the industry which are made to do P2V migrations. VMware has a free product called Converter. Quest SVG (formerly Vizioncore) makes a tool called vConverter and Platespin makes a product called Power P2V just to name a few. All of these can be useful in performing the steps described above.

So why do we care about this here, in a book about correctly managing a virtual environment? We care because *how* you do your P2V migrations is critical to a well functioning virtual environment. There is a right way and a wrong way to perform P2V migrations. If you P2V migrate the servers in your environment the wrong way this can result in processor scheduling issues and inefficient use of the virtual infrastructure as we will see in this chapter. In this chapter we're going to start out with how one should properly migrate servers into their environment and then take a look at how NOT to do it, along with the impact on environment.

Why are we discussing this here, toward the end of this book, if P2V migrations are one of the first things we do when virtualizing? Because it's necessary to understand a few things about how ESX server works before we can understand how poor P2V practices can affect the virtual environment. All of the things we've discussed up to this point in the book (memory management, CPU management and scheduling, disk usage, etc.) must be understood before one can really understand P2V best practices and the all important "why" we do things a certain way.

How TO properly perform P2V migrations

1. Capacity planning first
2. Pre-migration cleanup
3. After hours, full shutdown migration for critical apps and databases to ensure stable data
4. Exclude unneeded utility partitions
5. Split multi-partition arrays into separate virtual disks
6. Post-migration cleanup
7. Adjust VMs and guest OS's to single processor wherever possible (2 exceptions)
8. Remove unneeded applications
9. Review virtual hardware assignments

Capacity Planning First

As we begin the process of migrating physical systems into the virtual environment the first step we should take is to do some sort of capacity planning for the new virtual environment. Capacity planning allows us to figure out how much hardware we will need in our ESX servers to run the virtual machines once virtualized. In other words, if I have 100 physical servers that I plan to migrate into the virtual environment, I need to know how much hardware I will need in the ESX servers to run all of those environments in a virtual machine.

Note that the hardware I will need in the ESX servers is not a 1:1 ratio with the hardware I may have in my physical servers. For example, our company may have an IT policy of purchasing all physical servers with a minimum of 4GB of RAM, many of those servers however may not use anywhere near their 4GB of RAM. I could have a DHCP server that only needs about 768MB of RAM because that's all it really uses. This brings up an important point, *as we assign virtual hardware to VMs we want to assign what the VM actually needs not some fixed corporate amount.* This requires a paradigm shift from the way we allocate hardware in a non-virtual (physical) environment wherein minimum hardware configurations are often policy. I have actually seen IT departments carry that same old mentality over to their virtual environment and build VMs with fixed, large amounts of RAM and multi processor because that's how they purchased hardware pre-virtualization. This is wasteful and can create inefficiently configured ESX servers.

So if we shouldn't simply use a 1:1 hardware allocation between the physical:virtual environments how do we know how much hardware to allocate. This is what capacity planning is all about. The rule is, allocate what you *need* for the VMs, not what the physical servers currently have installed. To do this we need to determine how much disk space a server *uses*, how much RAM a server *uses* and how much processor a server *uses*. Consider the following example:

Capacity Planning for a DHCP Server – How much Hardware do we have?

How much virtual hardware do we need for the VM???

DHCP Server
- **Mirrored 72GB drives (72GB capacity)**
- **4GB RAM Installed**
- **Two Processors**

In this example we see how much hardware the physical server has but not how much it's actually using. Duplicating this hardware configuration in virtual hardware is unnecessary and wasteful.

Capacity Planning for a DHCP Server – The WRONG way, allocating what you have

DHCP Server
- **Mirrored 72GB drives**
- **4GB RAM Installed**
- **Two Processors**

VM DHCP Server
- **72GB Virtual Disk**
- **4GB RAM**
- **Two vCPUs assigned**

If we allocate hardware 1:1 (physical:virtual) as shown in the example just above we will typically waste many resources in our virtual environment. With capacity planning we are concerned with what the VM needs for *use*, not duplicating existing hardware. In non-virtual environments companies may have minimum hardware configurations for servers because they don't want to "under-buy" and possibly make the server obsolete before its time. Also, in non-virtual environments if you didn't purchase enough server hardware up-front you can't adjust the configuration should you discover you need more hardware. For example imagine if we purchased a dual processor server for an application only to find out 6 months later that the application use had grown to the point where we really needed four processors. In a non-virtual server this would typically mean purchasing a new server and a painful migration process to the new hardware. To avoid this and other such problems with under-allocation of hardware, as an industry, we tended to over-purchase. In other words we purchased more hardware than we actually needed to make sure we had adequate capacity, room for growth, etc.

This old paradigm needs to be discarded in a virtual world. When assigning hardware to virtual machines we can be more realistic and conservative because we can always change it without much ado. If I assign 2GB of RAM to a VM and find out a few months later that application use internal to the VM has grown and therefore the VM needs more RAM, it's really no big deal. I simply allocate more RAM to the VM in vCenter and I've reconfigured it.

Let's continue with our capacity planning example looking at how much hardware the physical server is actually using and then assigning that, possibly with a little extra for spikes in activity and growth, to the VM.

Capacity Planning for a DHCP Server – How much Hardware are we using?

How much virtual hardware do we need for the VM???

DHCP Server
- Mirrored 72GB drives (72GB capacity)
- *6GB disk space actually used*
- 4GB RAM Installed
- *Server never uses more than 512MB*
- Two Processors
- *1 proc running 1.5%,*
- *1 proc Idle*

Wow what a difference. Look at how little the physical server is actually using vs. what it has installed. I've seen at least one industry study that showed average Intel processor utilization in LAN environments to be 5-15%. Having been in this industry for 26 years I can tell you I think that range is high. Millions of servers sit in racks all around the world barely running above idle. We don't want to bring all of that waste over into our virtual environment by failing to do a little capacity planning.

Now that we understand, for our example scenario, how much hardware the server is actually using, we can make a proper assignment to the virtual machine.

Capacity Planning for a DHCP Server – Allocating hardware as needed

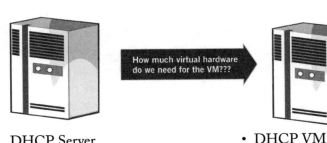

How much virtual hardware do we need for the VM???

DHCP Server
- Mirrored 72GB drives (72GB capacity)
- *6GB disk space actually used*
- 4GB RAM Installed
- *Server never uses more than 512MB*
- Two Processors
- *1 proc running 1.5%,*
- *1 proc Idle*

- DHCP VM

- 15GB disk

- 768MB RAM

- One vCPU allocated

What a difference huh? Compare the hardware assigned to the VM in this last example to the assignments made earlier where we saw how to do this incorrectly.

VM Assignment without capacity planning
- 72GB Disk
- 4GB RAM
- Two Processors

VM assignment with capacity planning
- 15GB Disk
- 768MB RAM
- Single Processor

With capacity planning our concerns are two-fold:

1. We need to understand how much hardware the physical servers are using so we can make conservative accurate assignments to the VMs
2. We need to make sure we understand what the servers are using so we can purchase hardware for our ESX servers that will accommodate expected workloads and allow for growth

Recalling that we need to understand how much hardware

we are using in our systems to do capacity planning, how do we actually do this? Well, for small environments an excel spreadsheet listing your physical servers and their key hardware components (memory, CPU, Network I/O and Disk space/I/O) can be adequate. Then simply use perfmon or whatever performance monitoring tool you'd like, to find out what the servers are actually using. Be sure to gather information over at least a few days so spikes\trends in activity and use (if any exist) are noted. For a small environment this method can be quite adequate.

For larger environments this "clipboard and pen" method becomes impractical because the task of manually gathering information on many servers could take large amounts of time and be prone to error. In larger environments it's best to use capacity planning software. How large is a "larger" environment? There is no hard number for this. It's simply defined by whatever amount becomes impractical for you to do manually. As an example, manually doing capacity planning on 25 servers isn't that difficult. Doing this manually on 125 servers however is quite another workload for an administrator. Doing this manually for 425 servers borders on impossible.

Fortunately there are solutions for these larger IT shops. Several vendors in the industry make software to assist you with the task of capacity planning for your virtual environment. VMware, for example, has a capacity planning tool that you can gain access to through a reseller. When last I used this tool, one would install it at the customer's site and the tool would gather hardware and utilization information from physical servers for up to 30 days. The reseller performing the capacity planning for you could then provide a report detailing hardware requirements for the virtual environment. You could also specify a target server configuration and the software could tell you approximately how many of those target servers you would need for the virtual environment. Search your favorite search engine for "VMware capacity planning" to find solutions for doing this.

Pre-Migration Cleanup

In any data center one can often find utility servers, applications and services that are no longer needed. It's useful, when migrating to a virtual environment, to go through the servers, looking at applications, utilities and data, and determine if there exists anything that we simply don't need anymore and can therefore remove. I recall once being onsite at a company that discovered they had an entire server in the data center devoted to remote access via a very old, modem-based, dial-in software application. They hadn't used the server in years since they adopted a VPN for remote access. This of course would be a great candidate for pre-migration cleanup. If you don't need it anymore don't bring it into the virtual environment.

One final note here: Make sure you look through the environment for any apps that may not function properly in a VM. Some examples I've seen of this include pre-historic applications that have been sitting in the server room for years and still use parallel-port, dongle licensing and old remote-use applications that bind themselves to the video board. In the former case when you migrate to a VM the dongle is no longer visible, this breaks the licensing and therefore the app. In the latter case when you migrate to the VM the remote-use app no longer sees the driver for the video board. Instead, it sees virtual hardware and will not work. These are just a couple of examples. The point is, look through your environment for items that may cause problems once virtualized.

After-hours, full-shutdown migration for critical apps and databases to ensure stable data

P2V migrations typically be done either "hot" or "cold" ("hot" meaning the source server is up and running while we migrate and "cold" meaning the source servers drives are inactive and all files closed). Servers that do not contain or provide user access to data – utility servers – can easily be migrated "hot." Examples of these include DHCP servers, DNS servers and print servers. Servers that contain dynamic data, and particularly databases, should be migrated "cold" in an effort to be sure no data corruption occurs and the database is transactionally consistent. So how can I migrate a database server in such a way that all of the files on the drives are closed? We boot off of a boot CD. This allows the server to be powered on and connected to the network while keeping the data on the drives quiesced.

As you are planning your P2V migrations you should plan on migrating these critical servers "cold" after hours. For the utility servers that don't contain data, daytime migrations or automated "hot" migrations typically work fine. Quest Software's vConverter and PlateSpin's Power P2V offer powerful options for configuring P2V migrations and scheduling them to run after hours (so you can go home and let the software work for you).

Exclude unneeded utility partitions

Many server hardware manufacturers create small partitions (usually around 30-80MB) on the internal server disks for various vendor tools (I.e. hardware diagnostics and performance monitoring utilities). You do not need these in the virtual machines because the virtual machines hardware access is controlled by ESX server. You may chose to continue using these tools at the hardware level but will not need them inside of the virtual machines. For this reason you should exclude these partitions from migration into the virtual environment. Most industry P2V migration utilities allow one to include or exclude partitions and/or drives as needed during the P2V process.

Split Multi-partition Arrays Into Separate Virtual Disks

In the non-virtual world it has long been the norm to have drive arrays internal to servers divided into multiple partitions and/or drives. For example, imagine a Brand X server with 5 300GB drives internal configured into a RAID 5 array, thus giving us 1.TB of useable space. This array may then be divided as follows:

Raid 5 Array 1.2 TB total available disk space

Partition 0	80MB	Vendor Utility Partition
Partition 1	30GB	Drive C operating system
Partition 2	100GB	Drive E application
Partition 3	1TB	Drive F data

We've already discovered that we should exclude the utility partition. As we migrate this server over to the virtual environment we could migrate partitions 1-3 into a single virtual disk that will be separated by these three partitions. This is undesirable however for a number of reasons. First of all, configuring your virtual disks this way makes expanding space on a single partition more difficult. Second, when I edit the settings of the VM in vCenter I only see a single virtual disk. There is nothing to indicate that that virtual disk is actually broken into separate drives. Third, from a DR perspective, it becomes difficult to impossible (depending on the backup tool you're using) to exclude drives from backup. Most image-based, virtualization aware backup tools will only be able to backup the entire virtual disk. What if I had a drive D that I wanted to exclude from backup because it was all swap information? If I have all of this lumped into a single, multi-partition, virtual disk this becomes impossible with many tools.

For these and other reasons it is a best practice to split multi-partition arrays into separate virtual disks as follows:

Raid 5 Array 1.2 TB total available disk space

Partition 0	80MB	Vendor Utility Partition	> Excluded
Partition 1	30GB	Drive C OS	> Virtual Disk 1
Partition 2	100GB	Drive E application	> Virtual Disk 2
Partition 3	1TB	Drive F data	> Virtual Disk 3

Now, if I edit the settings or view the properties of this virtual machine in vCenter it becomes obvious that I have three virtual disks associated with this virtual machines. This configuration makes it easy to increase or decrease the size of a single virtual disk if needed. This configuration also allows me to easily exclude drives from backup or setup different backup schedules for different drives if I like (for example backup Drive C & E only once per week if they are static and backup drive F every night since the data changes daily). I can easily exclude drives from backup if I'd like or selectively sVMotion™ virtual disks. For these and other reasons, this is a best practice. Fortunately all of the P2V tools I'm familiar with allow you to split multi-partition arrays into separate virtual disks on-the-fly as you do the P2V migration.

Post-Migration Cleanup

This is arguably the most important phase of the P2V process. Post migration cleanup is a multi-phase process that involves going through the new virtual machines and getting rid of unneeded applications, adjusting VMs to best practice with regard to processor allocation (1 proc wherever possible..see chapter on CPU management) and reviewing virtual hardware assignments to make sure they are about right for the workload of each VM.

Adjust VMs to Single Processor (vCPU) Wherever Possible

I won't endeavor to repeat chapter 6 here, but recall the best practice from Chapter 6 – wherever possible, reduce VMs to single vCPU VMs to make scheduling more efficient. Also remember the two exceptions to this rule:

1. Whenever the application inside of the VM requires more than one CPU
2. When you do the "megahertz math" and find the workload of the VM requires multiple cores. Lastly remember that only multi-threaded apps benefit from multiple cores.

So after you've done your P2V migrations do some performance monitoring and make sure those multi-processor VMs are actually using multiple processors. I was reviewing an installation with a customer just a few days ago and when one looked at a number of his dual vCPU VMs CPU 0 was running a low utilization levels and CPU 1 was completely idle.

As a reminder, if you are changing a VM from multi-proc to single or changing it from single to multi this typically requires reconfiguration of the guest OS to accommodate this change (the HAL for Windows and the kernel for Linux). A number of the P2V migration tools (i.e. Quest Software's vConverter) can make this change for you during the conversion process so you don't have to come back after the migration and do it. On the other hand, if you have existing VMs that you would like to adjust regarding processor count, you can also use vConverter and other products to do a V2V (virtual to virtual) migration and have the tool make the change then. This is sometimes easier than doing it manually.

I've only seen it happen once but I have seen an instance where making this change caused the VM to blue screen upon reboot. As it turned out it was a known issue and fixable but as is always the case with major changes to any environment, *make sure you have good backups first.*

Remove Un-needed Applications

You might ask, didn't we get rid of old unused applications in the pre-migration cleanup? Where possible, yes. But there may be applications that we couldn't delete until virtualized. A primary example of this are the many vendor-provided, hardware diagnostic and performance monitoring tools, many of which require direct control of and interaction with the hardware. Remember, we may continue to use these at the bare-metal or ESX levels, but we don't need these inside of virtual machines. Think about it: If you own HP servers and you have these types of tools installed, when you migrate those servers to VMs the tools become useless in many cases inside of the VM. Why? Because the VM no longer sees your HP hardware, it only sees virtual hardware. So let's remove unnecessary apps and tools from the virtual machines.

Review Virtual Hardware Assignments

In the non-virtual world we purchased software and by definition the OS was limited to the hardware of the box on which it was installed. In a virtual environment we assign hardware to VMs. When we do this the assignment is most often a best-guess. For example, if I assign 4GB of RAM to a VM, presumably I think that VM needs 4GB of RAM for its workload. Always three things will happen whenever we make a hardware assignment to a VM:

1. We guess high and the VM doesn't need anywhere near what we've assigned
2. We guess about right
3. We guess low and the VM is starved for resources.

After you build your VMs its useful to go back and review the settings. Find out what the VM actually needs and adjust where necessary. There are many performance monitoring tools in the industry that are designed for the virtual environment that can easily help you with this task.

Watch out for Duplexity Issues During P2V Migrations
This last tip is less of a concern that it was 5 years ago but I have seen it rear its ugly head many times in P2V projects so it is useful to explain it here. Duplexity issues refer to situations in which two sides of a connection auto negotiate or are manually set to differing duplexity. For example, a physical server is connected to a GB switch and the server is set to half duplex while the switch is set to full duplex. When this happens "late collision errors" can occur either drastically slowing or sometimes failing the data migration portion of the P2V migration. Let me explain with an example

Server A is set to half duplex. The port to which it's connected in the switch auto-negotiated full duplex. This does not cause a link failure and does not bring the link down. One day we attempt to do a P2V migration. Data is streaming from the server to the target virtual machine as we begin the P2V process. Because the server is set to half duplex it expects to send or receive on its Ethernet connection but not both. Because the switch is set to full duplex it can send and receive at the same time.

So, as the data is streaming from the server a response packet comes from the destination VM or server to the source server. The switch "sees" the inbound data stream on that port but because it's set to full duplex it thinks "I can send and receive at the same time…I'll go ahead and forward this packet" (ok it doesn't really "think" that but you get the idea). The switch sends the packet. The source server which is transmitting data gets a packet from the receive pair of its Ethernet cable and it thinks a collision just occurred. It stops the transmission immediately, sends out a collision beacon, waits a random amount of time and starts the packet transmission again. The destination receives an incomplete packet so it discards it.

Ethernet is designed in such a way that if a network is properly setup any collisions occur in the first 64 bytes of the frame – an area of the packet called the preamble. This way, if we are going to collide we get it over with quickly and early in the frame. Collisions don't occur in networks where all ports are setup to full duplex. What makes late collision errors "fun" is that these collisions can occur anywhere in the frame. The server may have sent 1400 bytes of a 1541 byte Ethernet frame when the collision occurs. Now it has to retransmit all of that. This of course is inefficient. This is also why these are called late-collision errors.

The classic symptom of a duplexity mis-match and late collision errors is that the ETA to completion for any large copy of data will get longer and longer, often eventually failing. For example if you start a P2V migration and its says "estimated time to completion 55 minutes" and come back a bit later and it says "estimated time to completion 135 minutes" then come back once more and its says "estimated time to completion 245 minutes" and then eventually fails, the first thing I would check is duplexity mismatches.

To check for this problem you have to manually look at each Ethernet connection between the source and destination, including connections through intermediate switches, and make sure each side of each hop is set correctly and the same. You can have half duplex hop in the middle somewhere as long as each side of that hop is set the same way Only when there is a mismatch do late collision errors occur.

One might ask, how could this happen if the server has been up and running for a long time? Duplexity misconfigurations can exist in networks for years and go unnoticed. The reasons for this are:

1. A duplexity mismatch typically does not cause a link failure.
2. User/server traffic is usually small and "bursty" in nature. This means that there may be occasional late collisions which have been lessening performance, at least somewhat, for years but the impact was negligible.

When duplexity issues become obvious is anytime we try to stream large amounts of data through these mis-negotiated connections (i.e. large file copy or a P2V migration). If you rule out duplexity mismatches and you're still having the symptoms listed above (ETA to completion growing long and longer possibly to failure), check the port statistics of each port along the way (including server NIC statistics and switch port statistics) for layer 1 errors (i.e. CRC errors). You may find some of these errors on every port. What you're looking for is a much higher relative amount. For example, in a 24-port switch most of the ports have a few errors usually totaling .01% packet loss but port 5 has packet errors totaling 7%. This is a classic sign of a defective transceiver or crimped cable. Replace the patch cables and if that doesn't help, try a new switch port. One of these three things, duplexity mismatch, bad cable or bad transceiver will usually be the problem.

How NOT to properly perform P2V migrations
1. Don't worry about capacity planning...it'll all work out fine
2. Don't worry about pre-migration cleanup, just bring it all over to the virtual environment
3. Migrate critical apps and databases hot so we can have fun with data loss and corruption, transactional inconsistency and perhaps data loss

4. Migrate unneeded utility partitions into the virtual environment so we can waste disk space
5. Don't bother splitting multi-partition arrays into separate virtual disks. This makes expanding disks, DR and VM visibility fun and exciting
6. Skip post-migration cleanup. This wastes server resources and guarantees lengthy event logs, thus giving us more to troubleshoot

It should be obvious by now why we take these steps but I can't tell you how many IT departments I've seen just migrate everything over like it exists in the physical world. This of course leads to a sloppy (at best) virtual environment, wasted resources, CPU scheduling problems and lots of other "fun stuff." Let's briefly go over each "How NOT to" and see the effects.

Don't Worry About Capacity Planning...It'll all Work Out Fine

If you're not going to do some capacity planning in an attempt to accurately purchase new hardware the only other option is to "wing it." True, contemporary server hardware is always more powerful that whatever was available a few years ago, but "winging it" can mean we spend a lot of money on server hardware we don't need. For example I did some work with a large government organization in Washington DC a few years ago. Instead of doing capacity planning they just went out and grossly over-purchased on all of their ESX servers so they knew they would have adequate resources. I suppose that's one way to fly but for a business that is responsible to manage costs and produce a profit, it's quite wasteful. Capacity planning can help you avoid such waste as well as guarantee you have adequate resources.

Don't Worry About Pre-migration Cleanup, just Bring it all Over to the Virtual Environment

If you just P2V migrate everything as is with no pre-migration cleanup you will guarantee yourself lots of fun with broken applications that had IP or dongle licensing. You'll also enjoy keeping old spyware, malware and viruses around in the new virtual environment thus guaranteeing the same poor performance such infected systems had before they were virtualized. Yes of course, I'm being sarcastic to make a point. These are good ways to screw up your shiny new virtual environment and companies do this kind of stuff every day. Just say "NO!" to sloppy virtualization practices.

Migrate Critical Apps and Databases "Hot" so We can Have Fun With Data Loss and Corruption and Transactional Inconsistency

This is self explanatory. Many P2V tools advertise the ability to hot migrate any system. Hopefully they work as advertised. On the other hand, if I cold-migrate my critical apps and databases I remove all doubt and err on the side of caution. No one was ever fired for migrating a database successfully with no data loss, so why not chose a method that increases your odds of success?

Migrate Un-needed Utility Partitions into the Virtual Environment so we can Waste Disk Space

Those vendor utility partitions provide absolutely no value to a virtual machine. They may not hurt anything either but the definitely waste disk space. Leaving the vendor utilities loaded in the VM will also waste RAM and CPU while filling event logs with errors since the utilities can no longer see the physical hardware.

Don't Bother Splitting Multi-Partition Arrays into Separate Virtual Disks. This Makes Expanding Disks, DR and VM Visibility Fun and Exciting

Once again, this is self explanatory. If you migrate everything as is you're going to add work and complexity for yourself when you need to resize virtual disks and partitions. You will also be forced to always backup and/or move (I.e. sVMotion™) all of those drives at one time since they are all in a single, multi-partition virtual disk. You'll also never be able to simply look at a VM's properties in vCenter and quickly identify how many drives are associated with the VM. This means you "get to" console into a VM and look around every time you want to figure out how many drives are there.

Summary

I think at this point it's obvious that performing our P2V migrations methodically and in keeping with best practice will yield many benefits. Our virtual environment will run more efficiently, we'll waste less hardware and therefore lower our expenses for virtualizing and increase the ROI for virtualizing. In addition the environment will be more easily manageable and IT resources will not be wasted through improper allocation.

Proper P2V migrations are an essential beginning and foundation to any virtual environment.

Chapter 8

A Few Remaining Tips
(aka: Things that are important to know but don't warrant their own chapter)

In this chapter I'd like to "ice the cake" so to speak. Here we will go over some final technical tips that are important to understand, but relatively short in terms of content length.

Free Hypervisors and When They Aren't Free

There are a couple of hypervisors – virtualization platforms - in the industry that are either "free" or very near free. These solutions typically do not run on "bare metal." In other words, unlike ESX server which can be installed directly on your server hardware, these solutions typically are installed into another operating system which is itself installed on bare metal. So, when compared to ESX server, which is installed directly on server hardware, these other solutions have architectures that look like this:

Figure A.

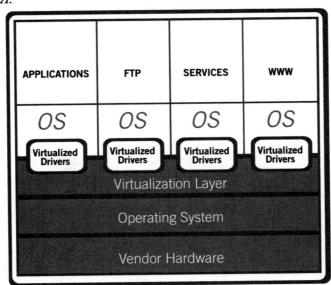

Notice that the virtualization layer runs on top of another operating system. On a number of occasions I have seen companies opt for these solutions thinking they will save money by not purchasing VMware's ESX server and vCenter software.

I'm sure you've heard the old saying "you get what you pay for." I personally have found this adage to be true in life. In virtualization, I submit, this old saying applies perfectly.

First of all, in this model, the virtualization layer and all of the VMs that run on top of it are all dependant on the stability of the underlying operating system to stay up. If, for example, you chose a "free" hypervisor that runs on top of Windows, how many in the room want many virtual machines stability to depend on the stability of a single copy of Windows running directly on the hardware? I'm not making any judgments regarding this question and answer, I'm simply submitting it for you to answer yourself.

ESX server is an amazingly stable platform and relative to other OS's that have endless amounts of security issues, is infinitely more reliable. I've been working in the IT Industry for 26 years. I've seen operating systems crash more times than I can count. After 7 years working in the virtualization sector of this industry I can tell you I've only seen ESX server crash a handful of times and in every occasion, it was because of a hardware misconfiguration or failure.

Second, most of these types of solutions are fairly limited as far as the number of virtual machines they can host simultaneously. It's typical with some "free" solutions to only get around 4-8 VMs running on the hypervisor simultaneously. ESX servers, on the other hand, routinely have 20,30 or even 40 VMs running on them at the same time (obviously depending on the underlying hardware). The VMKernel is very lightweight in that it consumes few hardware resources and it is very fast at providing VMs with access to underlying hardware.

If I use a "free" hypervisor in my IT shop, and I get up to 8 VMs per server when I could have used ESX server and had perhaps 25 VMs on the same physical host, did I really save any money? *In other words, if I have to purchase 3–4 times as much hardware to accommodate the low VM densities provided by my "free" hypervisor, was it really free?* Obviously not, so please keep this in mind as you look at virtualization platforms.

Last, ESX server and VMware software in general is by far and away the market leader in this space. This means inherently that there are infinitely more third-party utilities, monitoring tools, backup & replication applications, etc. for ESX server. "Free" hypervisors aren't very helpful when you have little to no availability of add-ons and apps for production and disaster recovery.

Relative Utilization

In this book we've learned a lot about the inner-workings of ESX server. Hopefully you've gained some insight into the mechanisms that keep all of those VMs running at the same time on your servers. As part of our closing comments I'd like to share a few thoughts on a concept that is particularly important to maintaining a health virtual environment, relative utilization.

In the non-virtualized (physical) world we had an operating system on a server and that OS supported any number of applications, utilities and services. As administrators of such servers we knew (or it was very easy to find out) how much RAM the server contained. It was easy to figure out how much processing power or network I/O we had available. Max disk I/O was easily discernable as well. In addition to all of this it was pretty easy to figure out what the average utilization was on that type of host.

When we virtualize, now all of a sudden we have 20-30 operating systems running on a single box. We are effectively doing time-division-multiplexing to provide fast access to processor. We are sharing network and disk I/O channels with many VMs. And we have lots of new RAM concepts such as shared RAM, VM RAM, VMKernel RAM, COS RAM, VMkernel swap, etc. We have proportional shares deciding which VMs get priority access to resources when there is contention for resources on the server. And all of this runs on servers that may have many processors and cores.

It's rare, given the power of contemporary server hardware, to find an individual VM that will max out a server, a disk channel or a 1GB NIC. It is important however, to understand the *relative utilization* of the VMs inthe environment.

For example, if we were to walk into an average IT shop of 250 VMs, we typically would find that most of the VMs don't do much with processor (low utilization levels) but perhaps 10% of the VMs, relative to the other 90% of VMs in the shop, have a much higher relative utilization. We would find the same thing with disk I/O. Most of the VMs in an average IT shop will have relatively low amounts of disk I/O (like DHCP, DNS and AD servers for example). But then we find that 5-10% of servers that, relative to the others, have a much higher amount of disk I/O (email servers and relational databases to name two). The same phenomena exist with processor and memory.

It's important to managing a healthy virtual environment, to discern the relative utilization of your VMs. As an admin you need to know which 10% of your VMs, relative to the others, use a lot of processor. You need to know which VMs use relatively high amounts of memory, disk I/O and Network I/O.

Why? Because HA/DRS have an amazing little feature that I have almost never seen used in any of the countless IT shops I've been in. In the settings of our HA/DRS clusters we have the option to keep certain VMs together and to keep certain VMs apart.

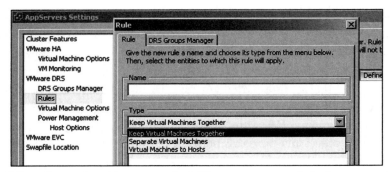

When/how should we use this? There are two subtle best practices here:

1. VMs that work together (particularly regarding network communications) are ideally kept on the same ESX server.
2. VMs that are resource intensive for the same resource should be kept apart.

Keep 'em Together

VMs that work together, and particularly if they communicate a lot with each other through the network, can benefit by placing them on the same ESX server. The reason for this is that the network communications between the VMs, if they are connected to the same virtual switch on the same ESX server, never need touch the network. These communications remain inside the server in the virtual switch infrastructure and the speed at which they communicate can be much faster than gigabit Ethernet. An example of this would be a web server that communicates a lot with a back-end data base server.

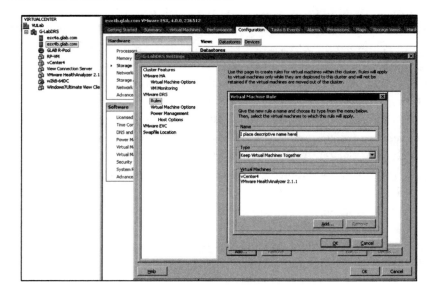

Keep 'em Apart...as much as you can anyway

VMs that are resource intensive for the same resource should be, as much as reasonably possible, kept on separate ESX servers. For example imagine we have an IT shop that has 100 VMs. We do our due diligence as administrators and we find that around 90 of the VMs do what most VMs do with processor which is, not too much. Most of these are hovering around 2-10% utilization of allocated vCPUs. We also find, however, that 10 of the VMs, relative to the others, have much higher levels of CPU utilization. They may not be maxing out a core(s) but if these VMs are averaging 30-40% processor utilization obviously they are using much more processing horsepower than the others.

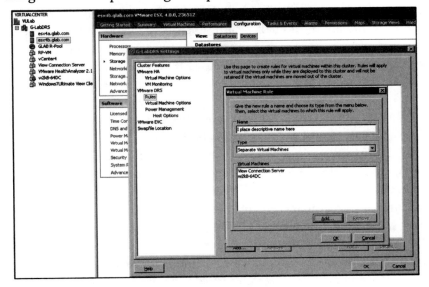

In this example scenario I don't want 3-4 of these relatively high CPU utilization VMs to end up on the same ESX server. Many people think that DRS is a load balancing tool. Well, it is and it isn't. It is in the sense that DRS will move VMs if performance gains can be had by doing so. DRS however, only takes into account a very few metrics in the ESX server. It does not, as of this writing, include such critical counters as CPU %Ready. DRS is not a load balancing tool in the sense that it does not sit there monitoring VMs moving VMs around to keep the ESX servers evenly balanced as far as utilization goes.

Having VMs that are resource intensive for the same resources ending up on the same ESX servers can lead to contention when there are spikes in activity. As administrators we need to know the relative utilization of our VMs and use these HA/DRS cluster settings to keep VMs that are recourse intensive for the same resource apart.

The Necessity of Third-Party Monitoring Tools

In virtual environments we have many VMs sharing resources, HA/DRS possibly moving things around and resource contention (possibly) on ESX servers . All of this exists in a dynamic environment where we can create many new VMs quickly with templates and clones, we can move things around with technologies such as VMotion™, sVMotion™ and cold migrations. To top it all off, we have many new indicators of health such as CPU %Ready, VMKernel swap, balloon memory, shared RAM, etc.

Even if you're an ESX guru and you know all of the critical counters, what they are, what they mean and where to find them, it's not practical to go through the entire virtual environment on a constant basis looking for all of these indicators of health. Even if we do, just because everything "looks ok" now doesn't mean it was that way three hours ago or that it will be ok three hours from now. This is a dynamic environment and we need tools that can monitor the environment 24/7.

In the ESX2 days Virtual Center had very few performance monitoring alarms build it. In ESX3 VMware improved it a little, but there were still very few alarms involving system health. In vSphere (ESX 4.x) VMware has definitely improved the performance monitoring capabilities of vCenter. There are many important performance indicators that can indicate there are performance issues for which vCenter has no alarms. vCenter is a great management tool What were looking for here however, is great performance monitoring.

There are many great performance monitoring tools in the industry many of them offer much more event correlation, diagnosis, expert analysis and predictive analysis of the virtual environment than does vCenter. As a virtualization administrator, you will do well to compare many tools in the industry that will monitor this dynamic environment for you and "tell you" when parts of the infrastructure are having performance problems. Find one that is specially written for the VMware environment and includes predictive analysis alarms, to let you know when resources will "run out" before they actually do.

Conclusion

In this book we've taken a look many common misconfigurations and mistakes that plague virtual environments. We've reviewed how to screw up your virtual environment and how to configure it wisely and according to best practices.

Imagine the virtualized IT Department that had a few storage issues (some incorrect allocation of LUNS and alignment issues). They also experience some performance degradation because their storage device is allocated as a single large array. Then imagine they also had scheduling issues because of excessive mixing of single, dual and multi vCPU VMs on their ESX servers. They also have a few VMs with balloon drivers that aren't deflating properly but no one knows about it because they don't have a performance monitoring tool to tell them this is going on. These VMs are being kept in a slightly degraded state of performance however, whether the admins know about it or not.

Hopefully it's obvious by now that all of these performance killers add up. The effects of these misconfigurations are cumulative. Any one thing may only knock a few percentage points off of utilization but combined together, the performance of this virtual environment is much less than it could be.

You can always find 1000 books to tell you how to do something. Rarely however, do you find books on how NOT to do something, how to screw it up, so that you can learn from the mistakes of others. Of course no such book would be complete without actually showing you the correct way to do whatever it is you are attempting to do. This book is that book. I hope this book helps you to avoid the most common mistakes found in virtual environments. I also hope this book helps you get the best performance possible out of the hardware you have, increasing the ROI for your investment in virtualization and assisting you in reducing problems in your IT Department. Happy Virtualizing!

Larry Loucks

Index

Symbols

.vmdk 18

A

Adaptive LUN 30

B

Balloon driver 62

C

CPU %Ready 6, 71, 73, 75, 76, 79–85, 110

H

Hypervisor 105–106

L

Local storage 16

M

Memory control driver 62
Memory over-commitment 61

N

Network I/O 8

P

P2V 4, 49, 71, 78–79, 82–84, 87–89, 95–104
pCPU 72, 75
Predictive LUN 30
Processor scheduling 71, 72, 77, 79, 88
Proportional shares 9

S

Shared RAM 61
Shared storage 17

T

Thick-provisioning 18
Thin-provisioning 19

V